THE INTERNSHIP MANUAL

THE INTERNSHIP MANUAL

A Step-by-Step Guide to Getting the
Internship of Your Dreams

Sharise S. Kent

Published by Divine Garden Press, LLC
P.O. Box 371
Soperton, GA 30457
DivineGardenPress.com

ISBN-13: 978-0692499023
ISBN-10: 0692499024
Library of Congress Control Number: 2015947728

Author Photograph © David McGill of DP Photography
Cover Design & Interior Layout: Divine Literary Services
divinelit.com

CONTENTS

Introduction		1
One.	Internships: The Icing on the Cake	13
Two.	Goal Setting to Get the Dream Gig	21
Three.	Setting the Table with the Right Resume	37
Four.	Becoming a Master of the Internship Search Process	55
Five.	The Interview Process	99
Six.	Paid vs. Unpaid Internships	123
Seven.	Get Out of the Comfort Zone: Interning Away From Home	131
Eight.	Becoming the Exceptional Intern	145
Nine.	Networking Doesn't Have to Be Awkward	155
Ten.	The End is Just the Beginning	177
Eleven.	Diversity	185
Twelve.	Action Takers	191
Appendix		195

he Internship Manual will help you understand how you can start your career making $15,000 more than your classmates when you graduate. Finding a job after you graduate is not going to be about your major, the number of clubs you led, your grade point average, or where you went to college. While completing your degree is a major accomplishment, all of the other applicants will have a degree as well. So, where do you gain an edge?

Ultimately, there is no *one* factor that will make or break a person's ability to succeed after college. There is, however, one factor that has proven to make a difference in successfully starting a career. If you want to separate yourself from your competition, get a financial head start, and be a sought after commodity when you graduate—complete an internship. To make yourself stand further above the pack, complete numerous internships. Start interning early in your academic career and complete internships as frequently as you can. Intern early and intern often.

According to the 2014 NACE (National Association of College and Employers) survey of recent college graduates, the average starting salary for students who completed a paid internship while in college was $51,900 versus only $37,100 for those who did not, a $14,800 difference. When considering expenses such as a dream vacation, buying a new car, or paying back student loans, an extra $14,800 per year would be a welcome addition to your bank account.

Between my sophomore and senior years in college, I completed six internships. While earning my graduate degree, I tacked on two more and a graduate assistantship. With each internship, I grew more confident professionally and personally. I was exposed

---

If you want to separate yourself from your competition, get a financial head start, and be a sought after commodity when you graduate—complete an internship.

---

to different types of co-workers and corporate cultures that would ultimately prepare me to understand what to expect as a young professional. I also gained mentors who were able to advise me on navigating the professional landscape.

Being a first generation college student, it is safe to say that my parents were not well versed in the nuances of corporate America. Although my parents were not white-collar professionals, they instilled in me other values necessary for success, including work ethic, respect for others, a receptive attitude, determination, and confidence. Carrying those principles through my internship and work experiences has helped me to have a successful and productive career. I have been able to combine all of my personal experiences, those in higher education, and working with students to write this book.

The Internship Manual answers the questions of how to find an internship, why they are important, and how to be a rock star intern. It will teach you how to get your first internship, be an exceptional intern, and then do it again and again. Intern early and intern often. It is a simple formula that can give you an edge, the confidence, and the connections to begin crafting your career before you even graduate.

Internships are vitally important for a number of reasons:

Gain Real World Experience. Completing an internship can help you build your professional portfolio, apply classroom theory to practice, and demonstrate real world results from projects you participate in—all making you more attractive to a potential employer.

Build Your Network. Building a network of professional contacts is critical to the success of professionals in any industry. A strong network will be an invaluable resource in the future job search process for potential leads as well as references.

Test Drive Your Career Choice. Gaining internship experience allows you to preview careers to determine if you are on the right career path. Before stepping out and securing a full-time role, get an understanding of what a career in your field of choice will encompass.

Get Hired. Employers like to hire known entities. Over the course of eight-to-twelve weeks, a company gets to know you and learn how you could contribute to their organization. If they are adequately impressed, they are likely to keep you in mind for future openings and not hesitate to provide a recommendation.

Meet or Exceed Expectations. As the competition for jobs gets more intense, employers seek ways to quickly weed out candidates who do not possess evidence of real experience. An internship enhances your appeal and demonstrates that you took your education seriously enough to complement your degree with outside experience.

My First Internship

My first internship was with the Rochester Red Wings baseball team. I started as a group sales intern and eventually became a game-day intern. I spent six months with the organization while they were the AAA affiliate of the Baltimore Orioles (they are now a part of the Minnesota Twins farm system). At that time, I was very interested in a sports related career, so I was looking for any type of internship with a professional sports team. I called the main office and inquired about summer internship openings. They told me the deadline to apply hadn't passed and that I should apply and submit my resume, which is exactly what I did.

I had just completed my freshman year at a community college while the other intern applicants were all upperclassmen at four-year schools. What helped me compete against other students coming from more rigorous academic environments and well-known institutions? In addition to a strong grade point average (GPA), good references, and a demonstrated interest in sports, I also had three part-time jobs before I ever had my first internship. I had gotten my first job when I was a junior in high school. By the end of my freshman year in college, I'd held positions at a movie theatre, upscale retail department store, and as a receptionist at a hospital. While those experiences were not directly applicable to the internship, they demonstrated that I was mature, responsible, and capable of adapting.

In addition to my previous work experience, my resume also showed that I had participated in athletics for four years in high school, including as captain of the softball team. Taking all things into account, I was a competitive prospect despite my being up against upperclassmen. Since I'd already been on multiple job interviews, when I got the call, I interviewed with poise and confidence. Beyond the paper statistics, I had to believe that I deserved to be there.

That first internship experience had me hooked. I was addicted to the concept that while being a student, I could also experience being in a temporary professional position. When you graduate and take on a full-time position, leaving after four months can potentially reflect negatively on you. Your next potential employer may wonder if you will leave them just as quickly. If you aren't able to provide a valid reason for a quick departure, it could delay someone else giving you a chance with their company. While you are a student and an intern, you get to try on as many different career hats as possible to learn, feel, and see what fits you and your career aspirations.

From each internship experience I took take away applicable professional skills and, just as importantly, life skills. They helped me learn about what I didn't want in my career, as much as they showed me skills needed to excel in the workplace.

Internships are not just about building your resume. Internships are about becoming more self-aware. Beyond adding new skills, approach your internship experience with the goal of achieving a greater understanding of what gets you excited professionally, the type of work you want to do, and the work environment and company culture that you can excel in. When you later start your career, you want to be energized about the opportunity to wake up each day, go to work, and be a part of something bigger than yourself. Your internship experiences will offer you great insight into narrowing down what type of company and what career you can be passionate about.

What have I learned eight internships later? I figured out that I didn't like being in an office all day; I wanted a career that allowed me to travel; I wanted to work with people who enjoyed what they did for a living (worked with too many people as an intern who didn't); I needed to be a part of something where I made a difference; and I wanted to positively impact people every day. I would have never learned these aspects about myself in a book in any classroom.

Professionally, when I started my job search, I felt very prepared and had the resume to prove it. As a public relations major, my experiences included internships in sales, marketing, business, public relations, non-profit, and government affairs. Combined with a solid GPA, good courses, a professional portfolio with real press clippings and writing samples, and great references, I knew when I graduated that I'd done everything I could to maximize my time in college.

One of my internships was in the public affairs office of the college I attended for my undergraduate degree. That internship was a turning point in my life because for the first time it made me consider working at a college, and the impact those in administrative roles on campus have on the college and the students. I ultimately started my career in college admissions as an admissions counselor for Keuka College, a small, private, liberal arts college in upstate New York.

Perhaps it was predestined that I started my career at an institution that has built a national reputation on the premise that internships and real world experience are keys to post collegiate success. They have a program called FieldPeriod™. FieldPeriod™ is an annual, self-designed experience that gives students a chance to explore their interests. A FieldPeriod™ can be an internship, cultural study in the U.S. or abroad, community service project, artistic endeavor, or spiritual-based exploration. Students are required to complete a FieldPeriod™ each year they are enrolled at Keuka College. Even if your college doesn't have a specialized curriculum that includes required experiential learning, you can still complete multiple internship experiences.

Becoming an admissions counselor allowed me to use many of the skills I learned in the classroom and during my internships. As a first generation college student, I embraced the opportunity to guide others through the process and found it to be an environment where I could be a difference maker. At that time I didn't know that I would spend my career in higher education, but my internship experiences helped me meet the challenges of a fast-paced profession and launch a successful career.

My career has taken me from Keuka College to three other colleges in undergraduate and graduate admissions. The four colleges I've worked for are spread across the east coast and include private, public, for profit, and non-profit institutions.

During my career, I also spent five years as the senior manager of the T. Howard Foundation, a non-profit organization that provides internships and professional development opportunities for minority college students. I have placed interns with companies like AMC Networks, BET Networks, CBS News, DIRECTV, Discovery Communications, ESPN, Fox Entertainment Group, HBO, MTV, the National Basketball Association, Showtime Networks, NBCUniversal, Paramount Pictures, Univision

Communications, Viacom, Verizon, and many other major media and entertainment companies.

In my time as senior manager, I had the privilege of overseeing the placement of over 400 interns across the country. Under my leadership, in less than five years the internship program grew by over 50 percent. Over that same period I directed the launch of the alumni and career development department to assist recent graduates with finding full-time jobs and advancing in their careers. T. Howard Foundation grew from providing top-notch talent for companies to fill internship needs, to working with those same companies to place full-time hires. As I said before, companies like to hire known entities and students with internship experience.

I have coached, counseled, mentored, hired, and sometimes fired students from colleges across the academic landscape. I've visited and spoken at well over 50 college campuses and have participated in countless career fairs and internship panels.

The information that I am providing you is not just about my time spent as an eight-time intern but the result of years as a senior manager, of working directly with students across the country from various colleges, and partnering with human resources departments at major companies to learn and understand their internship program needs.

Using my personal and professional experiences, this book will map out a path for you that can lead you to your own internship and eventual career success. Let's get started.

One

INTERNSHIPS:
THE ICING ON THE CAKE

ith the increasing number of college graduates every year, it isn't difficult for an employer to find a person with a college degree, good grades, and demonstrated campus leadership. The bar has been raised and the competition for entry-level openings is getting stiffer. In late 2007, the United States economy entered into the Great Recession and economic recovery has been slow. Companies that fired and laid off workers years ago have not rehired at the same levels. The weak demand for new workers has increased competition for entry-level jobs amongst recent college graduates.

Companies want to hire people who have already acquired some skills and experience. Many companies now expect that you have an internship on your resume. Since they have the luxury of choosing from so many applicants for many of the entry-level roles, students lacking in internship experience are easily eliminated as contenders.

According to a NACE survey of the class of 2014, "Sixty-one percent of graduating seniors had an internship or co-op experience." While the majority of students are taking advantage of internships, there are many who are not, leaving a lot of students who still have not gotten the message. Anyone who does not do an internship before graduation is putting themselves at a distinct disadvantage when it comes to finding a job. They are also potentially going to make less money in their first job.

Anyone who does not do an internship before graduation is putting themselves at a distinct disadvantage when it comes to finding a job. They are also potentially going to make less money in the first job.

Think for a moment about baking a cake. There are several ingredients required to make a cake, including flour, oil, eggs, milk, and cake mix (we are talking about making a box cake, not from scratch). You combine the ingredients according to the directions, and then put it in the oven to bake. When you take the cake out of the oven, it isn't decorated. If you wanted to, after the cake cools, you could eat it just like that. However, most people will take the time and the extra step to apply icing and other decorations to make it more visually appealing and appetizing. Also, decorating the cake enhances the flavor by adding a different texture and sweetness.

Now that I have you thinking about food, let's compare it to getting a college education. Obtaining your college degree is much like making that cake. You take the time to combine good grades, campus involvement, and leadership activities to make yourself a great candidate over 4-5 years in school. The internship is the frosting, or as the saying goes, "The icing on the cake!"

Graduating college with no internship experience is like baking a cake and failing to put icing on it. It may taste good, but it will be much harder to get people to try it simply because it doesn't look as good. Just as the icing serves also to enhance flavor, internships enhance your qualifications, making you more appealing to a future employer. The job interview process is the taste test.

If you graduate without participating in an internship experience you may:

- Be less prepared than your peers.
- Make less money.
- Feel less confident about your career direction.
- Have a harder time finding a job.

Completing internships in college is not a magic bullet that removes the responsibility of hard work and diligence. Doing an internship (more than one preferably) is just the process of adding tools to your toolbox. As you would imagine if you are working on fixing up a car, house, or other project, the more tools you have access to the better off you are and the more equipped you are. Internships position you to be better equipped to face the challenges of breaking into the work force after graduation.

Not Just Coffee

As companies have realized that there are bright and talented students on the cusp of entering the work force with something to contribute, internship experiences have gone beyond the days of making coffee and copies. Don't get me wrong, there are still some internship experiences that turn out to be of less value in terms of skill building, and unfortunately, that happens every day. As a whole, internships are valuable experiences that provide students with that ever-elusive real world experience that employers want to see.

Interns find themselves working on meaningful projects that contribute to the overall success of the company. The employer, for a time, gets an injection of a fresh perspective and youthful energy while the intern gets the experience. It can be a win-win for both parties. As an intern I wrote press releases and articles for the local newspaper, did research to assist sales teams in creating sales presentations, and managed the editorial production schedule and content creation for a parent magazine distributed to parents of over 10,000 students.

The projects I did over my internships were often engaging, interesting, and called on me to step up my game. Was every assignment I was given super exciting? Of course not, but there were incredible learning experiences mixed in with some mundane tasks. Eight internships and I never made a pot of coffee.

The T. Howard Foundation interns that I placed often provided value to their companies by engaging in activities that included things like writing press releases, designing website banners, pitching television show ideas to executives, monitoring production budgets, developing direct mail marketing pieces and email blasts, working on production crews for morning shows on CBS and NBC, producing advertisements, and so many other engaging experiences. Companies want interns who they can depend on to make an impact even in those short two-three months. The best internships will leave you with a portfolio of work and results to add to your resume.

Employers have basically begun using internships as a way to preview talent. According to the 2014 NACE Internship and Co-Op Survey, which included responses from 264 companies across more than 20 industries, employers made full-time job offers to 64.8 percent of their interns. What better way for the company and the intern to see if there is a fit than to make a short-term commitment? With this in mind, internships are viewed by some businesses as an employee test drive with the hopes of finding suitable, long-term hires.

In the last five years, I have observed a steady rise in the number of companies requesting interns as more companies became increasingly invested in growing their internship programs. The competition for the best talent is fierce. What has also changed over the last 5-10 years are the types of internship openings that are available.

In 2003, MySpace was king of the social networking world. The following year Facebook launched, initially for college students then becoming available to the general public in 2006. Since 2003, there have been a variety of newcomers to the social media scene including LinkedIn, Twitter, Instagram, Google+, Vine, SnapChat, and many others. These social networking sites have grown into million and billion dollar companies with consumer growth spurred on by tech savvy, young adults.

A decade ago, a position as Social Media Manager was rare and so were social media interns outside of tech driven companies. As companies began to realize the power of social media as a must have marketing and customer service tool, they also realized their more seasoned staffers lacked the understanding of using social media, thus the need for young talent to fill the void was immediate. Five and 10 years ago you also did not have internships in digital media marketing, iOS (previously iPhone OS) and Android application development, blogging, user experience design, and a host of other careers that technology has spawned.

The same way social media advancements drove the need for social media professionals, there will always be trends, technological advances, and cultural shifts that companies will look to young and fresh talent to help launch efforts. The creation of these new positions often begins as internships and eventually become permanent hires. Stay on top of the trends in technology and how they affect your industry. The insight and knowledge you can provide in an interview could be the reason you get your next internship.

Companies large and small are devoting time and financial resources to the development of their internship programs with the intention of attracting promising candidates for future roles. The application and selection process for some of the most competitive internships are similar to what recent graduates go through to obtain an entry-level position. Some internship candidates find themselves completing two-to-three rounds of interviews. The standard of what companies are looking for has risen to someone who could potentially work for the company, not just someone who will fill in a gap for eight weeks. Go into your internship experience armed with a game plan to stand out from the crowd.

Two
GOAL SETTING TO GET THE DREAM GIG

Plan of Attack

I t's 2:00 p.m. and you just got home after your last class. As you are searching the kitchen for something to eat, your phone rings. On the caller ID, you see the number of the company you interviewed with for an internship two weeks ago. You answer in your most professional voice, all the while attempting to keep your nerves in check. You hang up the phone and pause for a second because you are a little in shock that you were just offered your dream internship.

That could be you, but where do you start? It starts with a plan. There are five steps to getting an internship that we will cover in the next few chapters. An internship isn't going to just fall right into your lap. It will take work on your part to conduct a good internship search, send out resumes, and interview well. If you get good at finding internships, these skills will translate well to a job search when you are nearing graduation.

Writing your goals becomes a step in visualizing them coming into fruition. It may seem like a small detail but the act of writing your goals has been shown to be a predictor of success.

Steps to Getting an Internship

1. Focus and Goal Setting
2. Assess Your Skills
3. Get Your Tools Ready
4. Master the Internship Search Process
5. Interview with Impact

Focus and Goal Setting

Your goal might be to get your first internship, to get a more competitive internship, to get a paid internship, to intern in a certain industry, certain city, or with a particular company. Whatever you determine your goal to be, the first step in this process will be to write it down. Think bigger and be more specific than just saying, "I need an internship."

Writing your goals becomes a step in visualizing them coming into fruition. It may seem like a small detail but the act of writing your goals has been shown to be a predictor of success.

There was a study conducted of the class of 1979 Harvard MBA program students. They were asked, "Have you set clear, written goals for your future and made plans to accomplish them?" The results:
- 84% had no goals.
- 13% had goals but did not put them in writing.
- 3% had clear, written goals and plans to achieving them.

Ten years later in 1989, researchers contacted the group. The results:
- On average, the 13% who had goals were earning more than the 84% that had no goals.

- The 3% that had the clear, written goals were earning, on average, ten times as much as the other 97% combined.

Of course, there are other factors that would have contributed to the success of those individuals, but the simple connection of writing clear goals with a plan is obvious.

"I want an internship" is not specific enough. The more specific you are, the easier it will be to begin putting your plan together. You are also less likely to get distracted when you are focused and have a goal in mind.

Let's say your friend Brianna tells you, "I want to go to New York," and you have another friend, Landon, tell you, "I'm going to fly to New York for my birthday to go to a concert at Madison Square Garden, and then spend two days just touring the city." Based on their statements alone, who do you think is actually going to get to New York?

Neither one of them has actually planned their trip, bought a ticket, or booked a hotel, but because Landon seems to have a more specific goal, most people would believe his statement over Brianna's. Landon gave you a time frame (his birthday), approximate length of stay, and the activities he plans to do. When he sits down to make his itinerary, he is working from a solid starting point. The only thing Brianna knows is that she wants to go to New York.

Setting specific goals can get you thinking in very clear terms so that you will be able to have an effective internship search. Why do you want to work in that area or for that company? The answer could be as simple as you just want to know what it's like to spend every day in that environment. Alternatively, it could be more complex such as you could be trying to decide if you want to keep moving forward with your current major and an internship will help you decide.

If you are still a little unclear about your goal for an internship, here are a few questions to get your wheels turning. Answering these questions can help you put a few things in perspective while trying to identify your goal. Don't just answer them in your head. Grab a pen and paper, phone, your tablet or iPad, and write down your answers.

1. Do you want an internship that will focus on your major, or are you interested in exploring another area?
2. Is there a particular area you have an interest in learning more about as a career?
3. What type of skills do you want to gain as a result of this internship?
4. Is this your first internship? If not, what are you looking for to be different about this experience?

5. Does it matter if you are at a larger or well-known company? Will you be satisfied with a smaller, local company or organization?
6. Do you want to intern close to home, or are you prepared financially to do an internship in another city?

After answering those questions, the specific goal that you create may look something like these:

- I want to do a summer internship in social media that will expose me to how social media is used in a professional setting.
- I want to intern in the graphic design department of a mid- to large-sized advertising agency in New York, Chicago, or Los Angeles.
- I want to intern at an accounting firm in the forensic accounting department because my goal is to be a forensic accountant for the FBI.
- I want to intern at CNN in a news related placement because my goal is to be a news anchor when I graduate.
- I want to do an internship in research to determine if I want to teach or change my major.
- I want to intern in sales and marketing for any company.

Your goal establishes your baseline for your search. As you get into the search process, your goal may change, as what you discover about yourself and your interests may change.

Assess Your Skills

As you focus on your internship goal, the next step will be to assess your skills to see if you are qualified for that role. If the internship isn't in your major, will you need to take a class, start a blog, or join a campus organization to beef up your resume? Even though you are applying for an internship, if it is a competitive internship, you will be competing against other students who may be better suited for the role based on their academic background and previous experiences.

How do you compete for an internship in an area that isn't your major? Maybe you are a history major with an interest in marketing. How can you compete with the business and marketing majors for a marketing internship? That will come with some understanding of knowing what marketing includes and figuring out your transferable skills.

Transferable skills are skills you have acquired by participating in activities such as jobs, clubs, sports, hobbies, or volunteering that are applicable to another job. Some common transferable skills include public speaking, research, event planning, and leadership skills. If you think of the collective experiences you have had while in college, you probably have a set of transferable skills that you can demonstrate on your resume. Learning to identify your transferable skills will help you stand out as a candidate to potential employers. It will also give you confidence to apply to other opportunities that you may not have known you are qualified for.

In the field of marketing there are internships that are dedicated to market research. Generally speaking, history majors tend to do a lot of reading, research, have an appreciation of cultures and trends, and possess the ability to analyze large sets of data. These transferable traits are all great building blocks to research in any capacity. Therefore, students who are history majors wanting to intern in marketing stand a good chance of being selected if they emphasize these transferable skills. The employers themselves may not even realize the versatility of a person's background without being shown. Sharing transferable skills gets the potential employer to focus on what candidates can contribute as an intern and the value they can add to the company.

My advice to a history student who wants to obtain an internship in marketing would be to take a marketing research course, join a student organization related to marketing such as the American Marketing Association, or take on a marketing role for the campus history club. Those things can demonstrate to a potential internship manager that you are serious about your interest and pursuit of a marketing internship. Depending on the time of year, you could also look into working with a smaller company or campus department to get a fall or spring internship in marketing, and then go after a more competitive summer internship if you still believe you want to pursue that path.

These same strategies can apply to any liberal arts major who desires an internship in a different field. In addition to emphasizing transferable skills and extracurricular activities, another option is to add a minor that will boost your marketability for internships and jobs after college. For example, a liberal arts major looking for an internship in a technical or business field could:

- Join a related club or professional organization to learn and demonstrate interest (professional organizations such as the American Marketing Association, National Society of Hispanic Engineers, Public Relations Student Society of America, etc.).
- Move into a leadership role that demonstrates a new skill in an organization you are already affiliated with.
- Volunteer in a related campus office or community non-profit organization.
- Take classes in the subject area.
- Add a minor.

- Take technical classes that might be offered for free or low cost on campus or in the community to become a power user of software programs like Microsoft Word, Excel, PowerPoint, and Access. (Check with your campus instructional services department.)

As you continue to assess your skills you will realize that you are equipped to do more than you may have first thought. Visit your university's career services office; they can assist you with evaluating your past experiences to craft a resume that properly demonstrates your versatility as a prospective intern. Pay attention to your list of transferable skills; see which skills seem to come more naturally, those that you enjoy as well as those you want to improve.

Knowing yourself and your skills can help you be confident if you are going after an especially competitive internship. Being mindful of how you may stack up to the competition is helpful. With the overwhelming numbers of applications some companies receive, they have the option to be extremely picky and seek out the exact skills they desire. Each year glassdoor.com compiles a list of the 25 highest rated internship companies.

According to their 2015 survey, the top five highest rated internship companies are:
1. Facebook

2. Chevron
3. Google
4. Quicken Loans
5. Ebay

Beyond those companies, there are many others that will receive hundreds (sometimes thousands) of applications per opening. Consider how many sports enthusiasts want to work for ESPN or the National Football League, or how many aspiring journalists are preparing themselves to intern for CNN, MSNBC, or the New York Times. If you think it is a hot spot, then others are probably going to jump at the same opportunity.

If you are going after an internship that will be competitive, assess your skills. The students who are able to land these roles are often those who have a demonstrated interest in the internship area, have solid academic performance, previous relevant internship experience, campus or volunteer activities, and they interview very well. The top companies aren't necessarily going to hire only students with 4.0 GPAs. They tend to look for the intangibles that can make a student stand out. Projects they have completed, previous positions, leadership, and a go-getter attitude that shows initiative.

Doing your research on the culture of the company and reading about the experiences of past interns will help you learn if you are the type of candidate that would be a good fit for any company you have in mind. No matter if it is the first internship or you fifth, you have to take the time to understand who you are, what you want to learn, and what you have to offer. It will make your search line up with your goals and prepare you to seek out the opportunities that will put you closer to your dream internship.

Set Goals but Be Open

Although I've just spent the last few pages explaining the importance of setting a goal, I must back up momentarily and emphasize that you should also remain flexible. More frequently than you can imagine, I have contacted students about an internship for a major media company only to have them decline because they preferred to work with a different company. Almost 100 percent of the time they hadn't even interviewed with the other company yet. I was calling to offer a chance for an interview and they were declining a prospective offer for a call that may not have ever come. There comes a point when you have to know when to seize the opportunity even if isn't the dream internship you set out to get. You don't want to end up with no internship at all because your sights were so focused on one opening that you didn't see the benefit in another.

A great example that comes to mind is a student I worked with a few years ago. I contacted her during the spring of her junior year at Vanderbilt University where she was pursuing her Bachelor's degree in Communications with minors in Corporate Strategy and Sociology. Her career goal was to become a broadcast journalist, and she had already completed a few journalism related internships.

The company I was working to find an intern for wanted candidates with outgoing personalities, who could work well with others, was organized, and had strong communication skills. She fit the criteria; however, the internship had nothing to do with broadcast journalism. When I told her I was calling about a paid internship in Los Angeles in Human Resources, she didn't hesitate to seize the opportunity to move forward in the process. Her resume was sent to Time Warner Cable. She interviewed and was offered the internship.

Her duties included doing research, participating in career fairs, and working on team projects. Although she was not working on camera, she used her time at Time Warner Cable to understand the hiring process of a major corporation, network, conduct informational interviews, and diversify her resume. By the time she graduated, she had completed eleven internships, most of them in the television field.

She went on to start her career as a morning reporter for a station in Michigan and currently is a nightly news reporter for a television news station in Jacksonville, FL. Taking an internship in human resources didn't slow her down and obviously didn't keep her from reaching her dreams. She is a true example of what it means to intern early and intern often.

Getting Your Tools Ready

After you have identified your internship goal and evaluated your current skills, your next step will be to start gathering the materials you need to apply and compete for your dream internship. Earlier we talked about making a cake in relation to the role of your internship to your degree. Now that you've baked the cake, you are ready to dive in and have a taste.

Previously I said that the internship is the icing on the cake. Well, before you can dive into that great tasting cake, you need to get some utensils together and set the table to eat. Most commonly you are going to grab a plate, a knife, a fork, and a napkin. These are all necessary items that go into making sure you have an enjoyable dining experience. If you were given just a knife, you could use your hands but would probably end up making a mess. Having the right tools can make even simple jobs easier.

Translating this over into the world of internships, you have to set the table with the proper utensils, or tools, that will assist you in having a more successful internship search and experience. If you can take the time to set the table with the right tools before you start trying to find and secure an internship, it will make it easier for you. There are some tools that you will need that are tangible, while other tools are intangible.

Your tools will include your:
- Education
- Resume
- Interviewing skills
- Network
- Professional experiences

When used together, properly and professionally, these individual tools set the table for your internship success. We covered the first three steps to getting an internship. In Chapters 4 and 5 we will cover the remaining steps.

Three
SETTING THE TABLE WITH THE RIGHT RESUME

The Anatomy of a Resume

Your resume is the most important tool in your search for an internship. A resume provides a snapshot or written summary of your personal, educational, and professional qualifications for a job. It's your work history, skills, and education summed up in one neat 8½ x 11 inches piece of paper. Very often, especially when applying online, your resume has to speak for you before you have a chance to connect with a real person, which is why it is so important.

There are several basic types of resume formats, including chronological, functional, combination, and targeted. There are books dedicated to resumes that include hundreds of layout samples that you can refer to. The chronological resume is the most common format recommended by resume writers and career professionals for current college students. Most resumes are skimmed by hiring professionals in less than 10 seconds, so it is imperative that the most important information is easy to read and recognize quickly, which is what chronological format does.

A chronological resume lists your work history from most recent to oldest, providing details in the form of bullet points about responsibilities for each position. It allows employers to rapidly assess your work

---

Your resume is the most important tool in your search for an internship...The chronological resume is the most common format recommended by resume writers and career professionals for current college students.

---

experience. The areas that should be included are:

- Contact Information
- Education
- Work Experience
- Activities/Leadership
- Skills

Contact Information

The contact information section should include your full name, email address, street address, and phone number. Your email address should be professional. You may have an email address that you have had since high school that is more casual, which is fine for communicating with your friends, but is not appropriate for correspondence with a prospective employer. If you do not have a professional email address, as soon as you are done with this chapter create a new account. Some combination of your first, middle, and/or last name is appropriate. If you have a really common name, you may need to add a number, period, or underscore to your combination to create your email address.

Stay away from email addresses that include song lyrics, sports teams, hobbies, nicknames, popular sayings, sexual vulgarities, gender or race specific, politics, or anything that tries to be too funny or philosophical. Keep the more entertaining email address for your friends. Simple wins in this case so use some variation of your name or initials and play it safe.

There are various services that offer free email accounts. I recommend creating a Gmail account because it will also give you access to Google Docs for free. Google Docs will allow you to store your resume online for quick and easy access from anywhere. As long as you are a student, you can also use your school email address for professional correspondence. If you are a senior, make sure to check to see how long your school address will be accessible after graduation. If you won't have access to it long after graduation, creating a new account for professional purposes is suggested. Many schools offer alumni email addresses as well that can be used after you graduate.

If you attend school in one city and have a permanent residence in another city, it is okay to include both addresses on your resume. It could help especially if looking for an internship in a different city. You would simply label one as your "Current Address" and the other as your "Permanent Address."

Education

The education section of your resume will include your academic achievements. The name of your school with the city and state, expected graduation date, and degree program should be listed. In terms of a GPA, I highly recommend that you do not include your cumulative GPA if it is under a 3.0/4.0. It is also perfectly fine to not include your GPA no matter how high or low it is if this information is not requested in the job/internship notice.

Other items that could also be found in the education section would be academic honors/awards and a short list of applicable courses. Your list of applicable or relevant courses should be kept between three-to-five classes. Adding a few classes is a great option if you have a liberal arts major, but have taken courses that apply to the internship role you are seeking.

Since you are a current college student, it is not necessary to include your high school information or awards. As a college student employers know that you have completed your secondary education. They want to know what you have done since moving into the next phase of your academic and personal career. If you are a freshman or sophomore and you were Valedictorian or Salutatorian or you received some other honor, then you can include those on your resume. If it is not a unique achievement, it is time to remove it from your resume.

Work Experience

Work experience should be listed in order from most recent position to the oldest position. The section can be titled Work Experience or Internship Experience. If you have both work experience and internship experience, you can opt to create two experience sections.

Be sure to include the title of your position, the company, city and state, and dates of employment.

Bullet points are very effective for providing details about your responsibilities for each position. Visually the use of bullet points breaks up the text, making your resume easier to read. Using bullet points is not just about listing your duties, but each bullet point must be descriptive and provide insight into the task and your accomplishments. You want to use verbs, adjectives, and statistics to demonstrate how you had an impact and contributed to the company or organization. Your bullet points can assist you in highlighting your skills and bringing attention to what you want the employer to know about you.

For example, rather than writing: Gave customers information about store credit card.

Try writing: Top performing sales associate responsible for opening 20 new store credit card accounts in two months, exceeding store associate goal by 25 percent.

The second version provides a measure of activity and demonstrates results. An employer would be able to easily see that you can meet goals and are results driven.

If you have long embodied the "intern early and intern often" philosophy, then you may find yourself with lots of internship experiences and a lengthy resume that bleeds over onto a second page. As an intern, you should never have a resume that exceeds one page. The exception to this rule is for non-traditional students who have been in the professional work force for over seven years, who have returned to school. Outside of that scenario, you should not have a two-page resume.

When you run into trouble getting everything on your resume you can delete some information or create a second resume. By my senior year, between my multiple jobs and internships, I'd gathered a lot of experiences. I was hitting the limit of what I could fit on one page so I created a second resume. One resume focused more on my business and sales experiences while the other I used when trying to find internships and eventually jobs related to public relations and writing. If you make a second resume, just keep track of which resume you send to each job.

Activities and Leadership

If you don't have much work experience, the activities and leadership section is your chance to showcase skills you have gained beyond the classroom. Perhaps you have been active in a campus club, professional group, or volunteer organization. This section presents the opportunity to market those transferable skills properly to demonstrate your abilities.

The types of activities that you might list include your on or off campus involvements in clubs or organizations. When you list the club or organization, provide your role, especially if it was a leadership role, as well as years of involvement. If you are not involved in some type of activity on campus, I encourage you to find something of interest. Academic or professional organizations are great ways to learn more about various career fields without changing your major or to learn more about other career interests.

Between my part-time jobs and internships, I didn't have the time to join a bunch of clubs, but I did get involved with the Public Relations Student Society of America (PRSSA) and occasionally served as a musician for the campus Gospel Choir. During my senior year, I was elected chapter president of PRSSA. I didn't need to win the most active student award, but I knew it was important to engage in activities outside of the classroom and be a part of the campus community.

The companies you apply to will not look to see how many clubs or groups you joined but rather your commitment and level of engagement. If your school does not have a group that fits a deep interest of yours, start one yourself. What better way to demonstrate commitment and leadership than to create a group in which you can grow and develop to contribute to your campus community. Aside from the resume benefits, starting an on campus group gives you the chance to meet others with similar interest.

Skills

The skills section will contain a combination of your technical and language skills. You should list the computer software programs that you are comfortable using with a proficiency level of intermediate or above. If you include foreign language skills, you should include your proficiency level in that as well. Imagine for a moment that you speak a little Spanish so you put it on your resume. You get called for a job interview and the interviewer happens to be fluent in Spanish and decides to conduct the first portion of the interview speaking Spanish. What would you do? Save yourself the embarrassment. Take an honest evaluation of your skill set and proficiency levels before including it on your resume.

This section is also where you can list your social media skills. When including your social media experience, it is important to note that employers are looking for experience using social media for business purposes, not just as a casual user. List the social media programs that you are comfortable using for business purposes; don't just say "social media." There are so many different programs that you want to be sure to list the most popular sites that you have experience with.

Additional Sections

Many people maintain blogs and wonder if they should include their website addresses on their resume. I say proceed with extreme caution. If your blog is personal in nature, it should not be included. If your blog is a mixture of personal and business, it should not be included. If your blog is purely professional, consider including it.

For example, if you are looking for internships related to the fashion industry and you've been maintaining a fashion blog for years and have built a nice following, then consider including it. Make sure that all of your posts are professional in nature and don't touch on politics, religion, or other areas not commonly discussed during the interview process for a job or internship. If you are an animator, web or graphic designer, or other related artistic profession you should include a link to a portfolio displaying your work. Make sure your work is professional quality.

Now that you have all of your sections together, proofread it. You can take your completed resume to your career services office for assistance. If you are having trouble figuring out how to make your summer retail job or time babysitting sound more exciting and professional, a career advisor/counselor can help you understand how to dig around for the transferable skills that would be attractive to employers. Even as an alumnus you may still have access to career services at your alma mater. See Appendix A for samples of resumes.

Cover Letter

A cover letter is a letter that accompanies your resume, providing information about why you are interested in the position, and more insight into your qualifications. Cover letters are brief. Recruiters are often reading and reviewing so many resumes and letters that if your cover letter even looks too long they might not read it. Chances are that if you are applying to an internship online, their system might not even accept a cover letter. In that case, your resume will have to do the talking for you. You should still have a cover letter that speaks to your qualifications for positions that require one. Once you have your basic format, you can customize your letter for each position you apply to.

Header

The header of your cover letter should include the same contact information found on your resume. To simplify things, you can use the same header that you use for your resume. When addressing your cover letter, search as hard as possible to find the name of the person it should go to. If you can't find the person's name you can resort to using "Dear Hiring Manager" as an absolute *last* resort. Addressing a person in a cover letter would look like this:

Mandy Anderson
Internship Coordinator
123 Hire Me Way
New City, NY 11111

Dear Ms. Anderson,
[The opening of the letter should state the position you are applying for and how you found out about it. You can touch on briefly what qualifies you for the role.]

I was extremely excited when I saw the recent posting on your website for a Marketing Intern. I know that if given the opportunity I can excel at this position. Based on the skills and experiences I have acquired through my previous positions and coursework as a Marketing major at Towson University, I am confident and ready to take on the challenge of this role.

The middle paragraph(s) will touch on your hard and soft skills for this particular position. This is your chance to sell yourself, to show that you are a good fit for the role. You don't just want to repeat everything that the employer will find on your resume. You want to use this opportunity to provide more detail that you can't fit into that one page resume. Here is the chance to convey the important skills that will make you an asset to their company.

Last summer in my internship as a Marketing Assistant, I worked closely with the Marketing Director to create multiple client presentations. I was a part of the process from start to finish, and was able to contribute new ideas and gain a firm understanding of how new clients are acquired.

As the Vice President of the American Marketing Association student group on my campus, I've been able to share my passion for the profession with others. In my term as Vice President, I recruited an additional 25 active members to the organization and created a workshop on careers in marketing.

The next paragraph demonstrates your knowledge about the company based on some research that you have done.

In reading about the recent proposed merger between Time Warner Cable and Charter Communications, I know that this is an exciting time to be a part of Charter Communications. It would be a unique experience to see from the inside view how two major brands come together to create a larger, successful company. I would eagerly approach this internship with the right attitude of learning and contributing.

The closing paragraph should be a strong summary. It will suggest a meeting or an opportunity to communicate further about your interest.

As an experienced intern, I understand the importance and responsibility of being a contributing member of a team. I have met deadlines, created marketing materials, and presented to professionals in fast-paced, work environments. I am confident of my ability to be successful with your organization. I can be reached at (555) 555-5555 or via email at skent@company.com.

Sincerely,
Sharise Kent

Managing Your Social Media Image

For most people, social media is a large part of everyday life. Companies use social media to market their products, send coupons, solicit customer feedback, and update consumers on company information. In this digital age, it is important for you to realize that once images, messages, and statements are shared via social media, it is nearly impossible to remove them permanently. Once it is out there, there is no taking it back, so it is imperative that you are aware and diligent in protecting your social media image.

Legal or not, many employers will conduct searches on Facebook, Twitter, Instagram, Google, and other sites before calling a candidate for an interview. If a potential employer were to conduct a Google search on you, what would they discover? If a prospective employer viewed your Facebook page, would there be something that would give them reason to not call? Employers will tend to shy away from candidates with social media pages that they feel promote drug use, heavy drinking, sexually offensive materials, or violent

51

imagery.

Most sites have privacy settings that will allow you to limit who can see what. Learn how to set your privacy settings and monitor your accounts. Also, be diligent about who you allow to tag you in photos and posts. On Facebook, you can request to be notified anytime you are tagged in a photo. You might care about your page, but what about that friend who posts a picture of you doing something that you don't want shared? If you require notification whenever you are tagged or someone tries to post on your timeline, you can further protect what gets out there about you.

There may be posts, comments, or pictures that you have made that you might regret. There is no getting around it once it is out there, even sometimes after you take it down. In the event an interviewer brings up something from your past that was shared on social media, be prepared to answer honestly about the situation.

LinkedIn is a business oriented, social networking service used by over 300 million professionals. It is used to network, connect with others, and search for internships and jobs (or candidates). If you haven't done so yet, go to linkedin.com and create your professional profile. You should use a professional looking headshot (check out what others in your desired industry use). You don't have to spend money; just take a basic head shot against a plain background to get started.

Make sure you fill in all of the information you can, and it is super important that your profile stays up-to-date. Unlike your personal Facebook page or other social media, you *want* employers to find and check out your LinkedIn profile. It is a complement to the resume that you are submitting and the information should be identical. If you have a work experience on your resume, it should be on your LinkedIn profile. Your online profile allows the added ability to craft a summary, post projects, and have others recommend you. It is an invaluable resource available to you for free that you should take advantage of. Once you have completed your profile creation, you can add your LinkedIn profile address to your resume to make it easier for hiring managers to find you.

Regardless of the time of year, once you have your tools together, you can always get started in your internship search. If you are reading this book at the start of the summer, you can work quickly and find a summer internship or you can put these tips to use for finding an internship this fall. If it is already fall, start looking for spring and summer openings, and of course if it is spring, look for summer internships now.

Once you've created your LinkedIn profile, resume, and a cover letter template, you are a step closer to getting into the search process. If you already have your tools together, when you find an internship you want to apply for, you won't have to start from scratch. Your networking and interview skills will come into play during the next phase of your journey to your dream internship. Having a resume and understanding your goals prepare you to be able to network more effectively and interview more assertively.

Four
BECOMING A MASTER OF THE INTERNSHIP SEARCH PROCESS

So you have a plan, you have set the table with the right tools, and you are ready to start your search. How do you actually go about finding an internship? What is step one to figuring out where the internships are? To assist you in your quest, consider the following six ways to jumpstart your internship search. I have personally used or guided students in the use of all the included search methods, so I know that they work. Don't limit your search to just one method, but engage in a variety of activities to move you closer to landing your desired internship. To find an internship you can:

1. Ask around (i.e., network)
2. Visit your campus career services office
3. Work the career fairs
4. Think small and target local businesses
5. Search online
6. Leverage the power of internship programs

Prior to getting too deep into the search strategies, grab the notes that you took in chapter three when you set your internship goal. You will use the answers to those questions to start building your search. Based on those questions, you know what type of internship you are looking for, and have an idea of your desired city and size of company.

The students that made positive first impressions were always those who were dressed professionally, extended their hands to offer a firm handshake, made eye contact, and asked thoughtful questions that showed they had done their research.

Ask Around

It seems simple enough, right? Asking around works exactly the way it sounds. Another term that better describes what you are doing is networking. The Miriam-Webster Dictionary defines networking as, *the exchange of information or services among individuals, groups, or institutions; specifically: the cultivation of productive relationships for employment or business.*

My simplified definition of networking is about meeting people, and creating and maintaining relationships for the mutual advancement of all parties. Creating relationships when you network is not just about what you can get from the other person, but maintaining a relationship so that you can also be of service. We will explore the topic of networking more in a later chapter.

You may not have a large network presently but as you continue to have more experiences professionally and personally your network will expand. You don't have to feel as though you are not in a position to help anyone else because even today you can connect one person to another. In fact, if you sit down and make a list of all of the people you know, your existing network is probably larger than you realize.

To ease you into the practice of networking I want you to approach your college professors, department heads, and administrators and share with them your interest in getting an internship. Let them know what type of internships you are looking for and where. They may have professional contacts that they can personally connect you with in the industry you are exploring.

I landed one of my best internships through one of my communications professors who connected me to the right person. The contact from my professor landed me an on campus internship in the university's public affairs office. All I did was ask a person in the right position if she knew of an opportunity. Sometimes it just starts with letting people know what you are interested in doing. If you have done the pre-work before starting your search, asking around should be easy because you know what you are looking for.

It is best to approach your professors after class or during office hours when they might have a few minutes to speak with you. If they have some time, you can speak without feeling rushed. They could be aware of opportunities on campus or even connect you to an alumni in your field of interest. Adjunct or part-time faculty often has careers outside of teaching. They might just be looking for an intern to fill a role with their other employer or within their own business.

After you have gained some experience and are comfortable, begin to expand your network farther, don't just stop with the college campus community. Ask your friends, their parents, your parents' friends, mentors, and other professionals that you know as well. This is just one of the ways that you are learning to network. Don't be afraid to let people know that you are taking your education seriously and are looking for an internship to complement your degree. There are more people who are invested in your success than you may realize.

If you are not sure what to say, this is a sample script to give you a starting place.

You: *Prof. _____ do you have a few minutes so that I can ask you a few questions about internships?*
Prof: *Sure.*
You: *Great. I am excited about what I am learning here in your class and I am anxious to put it to use in the real world. Do you know of any internships that I can apply for? I am looking for a full-time (or part-time) opportunity that will let me see what it is like to work in _____ field day to day and that will give me the chance to work on projects and test my skills.*

All you have to do is start the conversation. If they don't have a contact right away, they may come across an opportunity later and think of you. You can have that same conversation with various departments on campus. Adjust the script and share with them what you are learning in your classes in general, and that you are ready to test yourself in an internship. As you begin to reach out to people who are not on campus with you every day you will need to call them or send them an email.

To start, make a list of all your professors, administrators, and friends who have graduated and are working in your targeted industry. Having this list to start with will help you keep track of who you talk to and how much of a reach you have. Add others to your list as you go.

You can create your own contact list by saving contacts in your email. You can also create email groups and label them accordingly. A better option would be to begin using your LinkedIn page. Connecting on LinkedIn will allow your network to keep up with what is happening in your life professionally.

A Networking Story

After receiving my Associate's degree, I immediately transferred to State University of New York College at Oswego (SUNY Oswego). I was starting my junior year on a brand new campus. Socially and academically it was like being a freshman all over again. Although I didn't know many people on campus and didn't yet have a large network, I knew I needed to act fast to find an on campus internship. Having already had two internships under my belt, I was anxious to keep gaining experience.

As I mentioned before, I approached one of my public relations professors after class and asked if she knew of any on campus internship opportunities. I shared with her briefly some of my other internship experiences and that I really wanted to work in public relations or communications. I want to share a little more about how the entire situation unfolded.

She immediately responded with the answer and directed me to the university public affairs office. She told me that they typically hired an intern each semester, and that it was a paid position (of course, I was thrilled to hear this). Later that day I marched over to the public affairs office and sought out the contact she gave me, the Associate Director of Public Affairs, Michele Reed. I informed Michele that my professor sent me over to learn more about the internship opening. We had a brief conversation and scheduled an interview. I went back a few days later for the interview. The public affairs internship was exactly what I wanted. I would have the opportunity to write articles and press releases, conduct research, come up with story ideas, and plan the annual community photography contest.

At my interview I was able to convey my passion and excitement for the chance to work in a public relations office. My coursework in public relations and interest in writing allowed me to develop solid writing skills. At the end of the interview, she offered me the internship. I not only had my first internship related to my major, I was also getting paid to do it.

I went on to intern in the public affairs office for my two years at SUNY Oswego. This experience led to my ability to amass a lengthy portfolio of articles, press releases, and press clippings. Having an internship at the public affairs office helped me hone my writing and public relations skills and was a big factor in my decision to pursue my MS in Professional Writing and got me to consider a career in higher education as an option.

In some ways that internship was life changing. Michele was not only my supervisor but became a valued mentor and friend. I used her as a reference for every job I applied to early in my career and she was one of the two people who wrote my letter of recommendation for graduate school. The process, that learning experience, the relationships all started with simply asking a person in a position to help, for their help.

Visit Your Campus Career Services Office

"Freshman year is the best time to go to career services so they can realize the resources available for career planning and have conversations about time lines and plans to have in place," says Dr. Marian Higgins, Associate Director of Diversity Programs at the University of Georgia Career Center.

Have you paid a visit to your university's career center lately? Often students make the mistake of waiting until late in their senior year to visit career services in a panic trying to find a job. They assume that the office is only there to help them find jobs when in reality they can help you with your internship search as well. The college career center (or career services) can be an exceptional resource for finding internships and jobs. Career centers have onsite interview days, employer information sessions, career fairs, internship websites, and vast array of resources at your disposal. You have access to all of those tools for free (well of course, your tuition covers this service).

Career centers come in different sizes and shapes. Some institutions have career centers/services for each college in the university while others may have just one centralized career center. You should learn and understand how your institution is set up so you can take full advantage.

"Career services offices have connections with employers and they come to us because they want to fill internship positions. We host information sessions from employers but if I don't know you are looking, I don't know to tell you about it. Employers come to our career fairs and other events too," states Dr. Higgins. Students have to learn to capitalize on the services and support they can have. Make yourself known to the career counselors in the career center and they can assist you with your internship and job search. Services such as mock interviews, resume reviews, career assessment

tools, and graduate school preparation are available to you as well.

Career centers are also a place to potentially *have* an internship experience. If you have an interest in human resources, marketing, social media, event planning, or other areas, talk to career services to see if they need your help getting the word out about their services to the campus community. Interning in the career services office can also give you the inside information on which companies will be on campus recruiting and what they are looking for. By helping out and playing host to the company representatives, you get to introduce yourself and make a warm first impression.

I have had occasions where students have expressed a level of dissatisfaction with their university career services office. If that is that case and you don't feel as though your needs are being met adequately, try and speak first with the Director to share your concerns. The result could improve not only your experience but that of other students as well.

If you need additional help in a more immediate fashion to find an internship, you can turn to resources on the web. There are books, online courses, and the option of paying for career coaching services. If you find yourself in that position, visit my website, www.sharisekent.com to see if my coaching services would be of use for you.

Career Services Success

When I started my quest for an internship for the fall of my senior year, I went to career services. Attending college in the small town of Oswego, NY, my internship opportunities were limited. I figured out early that local companies worked closely with career services to find the best candidates. My suspicions proved true as my career counselor provided me with a complete list of internships at local companies in communications and public relations.

If you attend school in a small town, it may take a little creativity, but you can find great internships with local companies. Even in small towns you will have hospitals, retail stores, city and county government agencies, newspapers, TV stations, and other businesses that want the assistance of interns. The difference is they may only have one-to-two slots available. If you do attend school in a smaller city, start early and you can get first crack at the best internship possibilities.

There are undeniable advantages to being in cities like Washington, DC, New York, NY, Los Angeles, Miami, Chicago, Atlanta, and Boston. Students in major cities have more companies to choose from with a greater variety of internships available; however, they also have more competition, not just from classmates, but from students at other local colleges as well. If you are in a big city you, too, should start your search early to get a jump on the competition.

When I looked at the list from my career counselor, I saw an internship with the New York State Power Authority James A. Fitzpatrick Nuclear Power Plant in their Public Affairs department that looked very interesting. I emailed the listed contact my cover letter and resume and was called for an interview. Clearing the interview was just the first hurdle in securing this position in what turned out to be a very insightful and interesting experience.

In addition to interviewing, once I got the internship, I had to go through a background check, psychological evaluation, and drug test. It was a pretty intense process. Landing this internship gave me the chance to work in the public affairs department for an active nuclear power plant. I contributed to the monthly employee newsletter, did research for press releases, compiled press clippings, and other less glamorous administrative tasks.

One of the more unique experiences I had while working there included getting to be a part of a live drill simulating a major nuclear emergency at the power plant. I spent the day shadowing my supervisor, the director of public affairs, in the mock command central where I observed the meeting of the top officials who determined what information was released to the public. It all started with a visit to career services and using the resources at my disposal.

Working the Career Fair

How great would it be if you could put on your best professional attire and go see one-hundred people in one place who all want to meet you, are in a position to give you a job or internship, and it won't cost you a thing? That is what a career fair on your college campus does; it brings prospective employers to you. Your school may call it a Career/Internship Fair, Graduate School/Career Fair or other name, but they all serve the same function—to bring professional and academic opportunities to students.

Most of the time the career services office or a particular college within a university will sponsor the event. If it is sponsored by career services, it will usually be open to all majors. If the fair is sponsored by a specific department such as the College of Communications or School of Engineering, those events will target those majors.

Employers attend because they get to meet a variety of students from all academic backgrounds in one place and make a personal connection. Students should attend because it would otherwise be almost impossible for them to meet so many prospective employers from across the country at once. If you perform well and understand the value in making a good impression at a career fair, it can open up opportunities that are hard to come by when you are just another application coming in from over the internet.

Beyond the obvious reason of looking for an internship or job, also consider attending a career fair as a chance to learn about companies and professions that you may not have previously considered, get advice from company recruiters on how to stand out, and to network.

The fairs generally take place during the fall semester between September – November or in the spring between February – April. Some institutions will have both fall and spring fairs. Look for signs, emails, and posters around campus advertising the event.

After 15 years in higher education and career development, I have worked hundreds of college, internship, graduate school, and career fairs. I've enjoyed the chance to travel the country and visit universities from east to west coast and engage face to face with energetic, bright, and eager students. At most events there have always been a handful of students who have left a lasting impression on me.

Considering the number of events I've worked, saying that only a handful of students per event stood out must mean that there were many students who failed to make a lasting impression. The reason is that most students do not understand how to "work" a career fair. They don't have a game plan and they cease to take full advantage of the opportunity to get face-to-face contact with hiring professionals. The hiring professionals at these events are human resources coordinators, department managers, recruiters, and other people who are constantly looking for talent to add to their companies.

What should your plan be to make the most of the college fair? First, some schools will make the list of attendees available beforehand. If so, visit the career center in person or online and obtain that list. Identify the companies that seem most appealing and visit their websites and read articles to get an understanding of their internship and entry-level careers. Doing a bit of research can help you stand out by giving you the information and confidence to sound knowledgeable about their business when you start a conversation with the representative. If you can't get a list beforehand, ask one of the career counselors in career services if they can share with you what companies will be there.

When you arrive, after you register, make sure to check out the layout of the space and where your targeted companies are located. There will probably be lots of tables set up with representatives behind or beside their table attempting to attract you with huge displays and free giveaways. If you have the time, it is okay to do a quick walk thru to see who is there. Although you may have obtained a list, sometimes things happen and the company doesn't show or they could be running late (if you are very early). Taking the quick lap around can also help you start to notice companies you may not have marked on your list and map out the order that you will visit the tables.

Then it is time to get started. It is quite possible that your target companies might also be the same companies that fifty other people want to talk to too—and all at the same time. So, what do you do when you see a line? You can either choose to wait, circle around to one of your other target companies, or go learn about a new company that wasn't on your target list. Make sure to check back in when the line is shorter.

At busier events that I have worked, I've experienced what seemed to a never-ending line of students waiting to speak with me. Most representatives, myself included, enjoy those opportunities to meet so many prospects. Although you may come up to a line and see thirty students in front of you, stick it out, stay in line, and don't just leave or get discouraged because you don't want to wait a few extra minutes. The person (or people) behind that table are doing their best to give each person the same fair attention.

The students that made positive first impressions were always those who were dressed professionally, extended their hands to offer a firm handshake, made eye contact, and asked thoughtful questions that showed they had done their research. For students who were unfamiliar with the organization, I always appreciated that they would still ask good questions with a genuine interest in what I had to share. Whatever you do, don't just stand there looking at the table, ask a question and introduce yourself.

Even though you have your targeted list, there are a bunch of other opportunities in the room that you have the chance to learn about too. Do not become so preoccupied with a few that you fail to take advantage of the resources in the room. Just because an organization doesn't have name recognition, the display isn't nine feet tall with flashing lights, and there are no free giveaways, that does not mean that the company may not be able to offer you something of value.

Not every company is a fit. If you are looking for an engineering internship then working for a women's clothing store probably won't be a fit for you; however, you could ask a question just to see if they have a need for people with analytical skills. What harm does a question pose? Remember when we talked about networking not just being about you? Well, when you acquire new information, you then have something to offer someone else as a resource. Perhaps someone you know is looking for an internship in retail and you could take that information back to them. Part of networking and maintaining relationships is about sharing information.

Whenever you approach a company representative you can do a few simple things to make a solid first impression.

1. Smile. A smile goes a long way. By just being pleasant, smiling, and friendly you are already starting off on the right foot.

2. Offer a firm handshake. Don't just stand there and stare at the information on the table. Make eye contact and extend your hand for a handshake. Introduce yourself.

3. Have three to five thoughtful questions prepared based on what you've researched to show your interest in the company. If it isn't a company that you have researched, you should have three to five generic questions prepared for those companies.

4. Complete the company request card for information (if they have one).

5. At the conclusion of the conversation, ask if they are accepting resumes, and if so leave a copy with them. If not, ask how you can apply online.

6. Ask if you can have a business card to follow-up with them. If they decline or do not have a card to share, you can ask what the best method to follow up will be.

The person representing the company or organization wants to meet engaging and interesting students who might be an asset to their company. Show them that you have a warm personality and that you are someone they should want to get to know better. These are a few sample scripts that can help you get started with approaching the representatives at fairs.

Sample Script - Target Company

Hi, my name is_____ (while offering a firm hand shake). Nice to meet you _____. I am so excited to speak with you and glad that you came to this event at my school. I have done a little research about [insert company name] and I am really excited about the type of work your company does. I am a junior majoring in [insert major]. I want to learn from you today what I can do to maximize my chances of getting selected for your internship program. What qualities do you look for in your interns?

Note: After you say your name, don't just rush through and not let the representative say theirs. Try to sound comfortable and not over rehearsed.

Sample Script - Non Target Company

Hi, my name is_____ (while offering a firm hand shake). Nice to meet you. I am not familiar with your company but I would love to learn anything you can share with me about (name of company). I am a junior, majoring in [insert major], looking for an internship this summer in sales and marketing. What type of internship opportunities are available within your company? What types of skills do you look for in your interns?

Pre-Career Fair Checklist

- Select your outfit the night before. Make sure it is clean and ironed. You will find a professional dress guideline for men and women in the Interview chapter. The same clothes you would wear for a job interview would be the same appropriate attire for a career fair. Check the weather to see if you will need an umbrella.
- Get a good night sleep so you look refreshed and feel alert.
- Pick out your target companies and do your research.
- Prepare a list of five to eight questions so that you can change it up when you approach different tables

or if you get the chance to have a lengthy conversation you have more questions to ask.

- Be prepared to answer questions about your resume, your interests, and what type of internship experience you are looking for.
- Print extra copies of your resume.

During the Fair Checklist

- Get a list of the companies and the layout of the menu, and map out your plan.
- If your target companies have a line of people, check out another company and circle back around later.
- Don't monopolize the representatives time when you see others waiting.
- Make sure you speak clearly and loud enough to be heard but don't yell.
- Make eye contact, smile, and have a firm hand shake.
- Thank the representative for their time.
- Do not ask about pay or benefits.

I Found My Internship at a Career Fair

During my junior year I attended a career fair on campus at SUNY Oswego. While making my way around the event I came across the table for Enterprise Rent–a–Car. As a public relations major, I was very interested in working in my field, but I was still open to learning about other opportunities. I was open to having another sales and marketing internship to learn more about the practices involved.

What was the most intriguing about my conversation with the recruiter was that as a company, through their paid internship program they promoted the ability to understand how to learn to run your own business. I understood even then that business skills would be good to have no matter what direction my career took me. The position offered transferable skills and experiences that would make me more marketable in a variety of capacities.

Based on my conversation with the recruiter, I went back to my dormitory that evening and did more research. They had a creative career website that allowed you to walk through a day in the life of an intern. They also promoted management interns to management trainees if you did well. I was very interested and went ahead and completed the online application.

Shortly thereafter I did a phone interview and then was invited to interview with a branch manager. Ultimately, I got the internship. I worked for Enterprise Rent-a-Car for eight months at three different locations in upstate New York. It was a great experience to work for a large, international company, and I was exposed to a lot about business. I got to see and experience the company culture, career track, and growth from the inside. By stopping at the table for a company that wasn't on my list, having a conversation, and being open to opportunity I came away with another impressive internship and real world experience all while getting paid.

Career Fair Resumes

One of the things you should have with you when making your way to a career fair is your resume. Although you have already read about resumes earlier in this book, let's briefly touch on what could happen with your resume at a career fair.

In today's recruiting climate many things are done online. As a result, some recruiters might not accept your hard copy resume. Don't take it personal. When I was recruiting, I would have students attempt to give me resumes all the time and I would politely decline. Since the internship application was all online, there was nothing I could really do with a paper resume. Many companies have moved to an online only system and won't collect resumes for the same reason.

Now, does that mean you shouldn't take a paper copy of your resume? No, it doesn't. Some companies will take your physical copy and still require you to apply online. Sometimes the recruiter may take your resume to write a note to themselves about what you discussed so that when you do apply they can remember better who you are. Nevertheless, don't take it personal if they don't take your resume.

Career Fair Leads to a Job Offer

When I was a senior in college I attended the spring career fair at SUNY Oswego. Prior to the fair, I made my list of target companies that I wanted to speak with. As I was making my way around the gymnasium I came up on the table of a major retailer, Staples Inc. I knew Staples was a major retail chain that primarily sold office supplies.

As a communications major, I was more curious about potential corporate office opportunities in public relations so I stopped to learn more about the company. The recruiter was looking for upcoming graduates to enter their two-year management trainee program. The position would require a person to work at a store for two years rotating through each department and ultimately moving up to become general manager of their own store.

Although they weren't on my list and I was looking for a public relations role, I gave the representative my time and attention. She shared with me that although she was recruiting for retail positions that once within the company, I could later apply for a role in the headquarters for a position in public relations. We had a wonderful conversation which lead to me leaving my resume with her. In addition to me degree, my previous experience in retail and my sales internships made me an attractive candidate for their trainee program.

A few days later I received a phone call and we did a brief phone interview. A few days following the phone interview, I was invited to do an in-person interview at one of their stores. My interview at the store was with the general manager. It lasted about an hour. I remember one of the major things that we discussed was that in their management program I would be learning to run a business. Being interested in entrepreneurship, that was a very appealing factor for me.

The time between the initial meeting and all of the interviews was about two months. Graduation was nearing and I didn't have a job lined up yet so when I got the call offering me the job, I was thrilled.

I thought long and hard about the opportunity that was within my reach. After four years of hard work, six internships, multiple part-time jobs, extracurricular activities, and keeping my grades up, I'd gotten an offer for my first professional job right before graduation. Ultimately, I declined the position and I chose instead to start a career in higher education. Although I didn't take the job, the entire experience unfolded as the result of my stopping to have a conversation at a career fair with a company that wasn't on my list. The lesson learned is to remain open and flexible.

Think Small and Target Local Businesses

Not every meaningful and amazing internship experience has to come from a Fortune 500 company with 5,000+ employees. There are thousands of smaller companies with as few as 5-500 employees who gladly welcome interns into their operations. In fact, over 60 percent of American workers work for companies with less than 500 employees. Smaller companies and non-profit organizations can often be a great resume boost and opportunity for that first internship. More competitive internships often require previous internship experience or are reserved for upper classmen. If you don't have much experience or you are a freshman (or high school student) this can be a great starting point.

"I can attest to it from experience. My very first internship, after my freshman year of college, was at a small non-profit organization. I gained so much experience during that job, and it helped me attain internships at more renowned companies in the consecutive years." - Zara Mahmud.

I met Zara during her sophomore year at St. Francis College in New York where she was studying Communications with a concentration in Advertising. The experiences that she had at the small, non-profit organization were so substantial that she was the perfect fit for an internship with Comcast Spotlight. I contacted her about the internship, she interviewed with the company, and accepted the offer. She stayed with Comcast Spotlight at her internship for one year. The summer prior to senior year she interned with MediaCom. After graduation she headed straight to graduate school at Emerson College where she earned a Master's in Global Marketing and Advertising and while a graduate student she interned with Verizon.

Get creative and think about your neighborhood and all of the business that happens around you every day. Have you checked with your local family owned book store about their social media marketing, your local lawn care service that could use someone to help with their accounting, or an after-school program for elementary school students who needs help recruiting volunteers? Use your imagination and consider your current skill set and where you could be useful to a company or organization and what you want to gain experience doing. Be cautious however to not make promises you can't deliver.

Start knocking on doors. Grab your resume and begin to visit the local businesses that you would be interested in interning for. If you are away at school and will be back home for the summer, call or send an email with your resume and stop by on your school breaks. Let them know you are a college student looking to do an internship, you've done some research, and are very interested in learning how you can intern with their company. You may get rejected and you may get people who ignore you, but you may also get an internship. After you make the contact, hopefully you are invited for an interview and you can impress them enough to get an opportunity to intern with them.

Opportunity Knocks

One day early in the summer between my junior and senior year my mother instructed me to take a bag of clothes to a small non-profit shelter for women down the street from our house. Although I'd lived in the same house since I was born and passed by the building for years, I'd never gone in or even knew what was in the building. The old, beautiful building with the sprawling green lawn, was always quiet and always seemed slightly creepy to me. The building was an old nun's convent.

After my mother explained that it was a shelter for women, I was intrigued. I dutifully made my way to the shelter and knocked on the front door. Once I was inside, I started to ask questions about the services they provided and was taken on a tour. The Sojourner House is an organization that serves homeless women and children by providing housing, self-sufficiency skills, and education programs. Residents of the house work with a case manager to create a life plan that will allow them to find employment and eventually move out on their own.

While on the tour, I was introduced to the person who handled the public relations for the organization. I told her that I was a public relations major and that I was interested in interning with them so that I could learn more about public relations at a non-profit. We set up a time for me to come back and interview. I got the internship.

As a small non-profit organization they were not in a position to offer me compensation, but my aim was to gain more experience. They didn't have a formal internship program so there was some latitude in what my duties included. Now, since the internship was unpaid, I was only able to work two days a week, six hours per day. My other days were filled with two part-time jobs. That was my first non-profit work experience, and I got to see how smaller organizations work with limited resources. I have to thank my mother for making me take the donation of clothes to the shelter; however, because I had my eyes open, I was able to take advantage of the opportunity before me.

Sample Telephone Script for Calling a Small Company

You: *Hi, my name is_____ . Can I speak to the person responsible for your internship program?*
Them: *Sure (although you might be met with voicemail or given an email address, leave a message or write down the email address)*
You: *Hello, my name is _____. I am a [insert year] majoring in [insert major] at [insert school]. I've been researching your company and I am interested in learning more about your internship program.*

The person you are connected to could be the owner, manager, human resources person, or member of the staff. Many small businesses won't necessarily have an internship coordinator. It could be a little intimidating at first, but you won't know what will happen until you try.

Depending on the size of the company or organization it is quite possible that they do not have a formal internship program. If they don't, you can proceed to offer them a service you think they may be interested in; offer to solve a problem. *"I noticed that you do not have a Facebook page and I think I could be of assistance in helping you increase your marketing and social media presence."* The next question they ask could be how you intend to do that, so be clear on what you know how to do and how you can help the company.

If you are trying to create an internship opportunity where one does not exist, the company might not be able to pay you. If you need to work another job, leave yourself enough time in your schedule to do so. You might not be able to do 40 hours per week but you can work 10-15 hours and make a contribution, gain new skills, get a reference, network, and learn about a new industry.

Search Online

The days of searching newspaper classified ads for jobs are long gone. Nowadays there are online job boards and company websites that have taken place of the old ways of searching. You have probably heard of websites like monster.com, careerbuilder.com, and indeed.com. In addition to the massive job boards like those, there are also job boards that are dedicated primarily to students seeking internship opportunities (Check out www.internsushi.com, www.internships.com, and internmatch.com or conduct a search for additional sites.)

Company websites. If you know where you want to work, go right to the company website to create an account (if possible), view positions, and apply.

Online internship job boards. If you are looking for an internship, consider sites such as internsushi.com, internships.com, and internmatch.com to start.

Local newspaper websites. If you are looking to relocate for the summer, check the local newspaper or news channel website for internship postings in your target area.

Job boards for professional associations. If you are a member of a professional association, they will more than likely have a job board section on their website. If you are a student seeking an internship, check the website of the student version of the professional association. If you are not a member of a professional association, do your research and join one today (ex.,

Public Relations Student Society of America, American Marketing Association, Women in Cable Telecommunications, etc.). In addition to the job board, you may also learn about networking events held for members only.

Industry specific job boards. If you are looking for an internship in a specific industry there is probably a job board for it (i.e., idealist.org for non-profit opportunities). Do a Google search or ask a professional already in that industry that you are trying to get an internship in.

With so many online search options it can be easy to get overwhelmed. If you are able to start with your goal in mind, it will make it easier to get through the thousands of postings you can come across online. Online internship sites can allow you to set up profiles, learn about companies and the experience of other interns, as well as provide you with useful information to help in your search and during your internship.

When possible, if you find a company you are interested in and they post internships on their site, I recommend applying through their website as well. If you are applying to big companies like NBCUniversal, Comcast, the National Basketball Association, Facebook, etc., then you most definitely want to visit their websites. Visiting those sites will give you the information you need to know about applying and the processes involved. In most cases when you are going after the extremely competitive and sought after internships you will be up against hundreds and often thousands of other students (hint: catch them at a career fair and make a personal contact). With so much competition, is it even worth it to apply to a position you find online? Yes, it is and here are a few tips to do so:

1. Read the internship eligibility requirements to make sure you qualify for the program (GPA, class year, coursework, etc.).

2. Understand what they are looking for and make sure your application and resume speak to how you can contribute. For example, if you are an English major and you are applying to a business internship, you have to demonstrate through your resume that you have the right experiences through other avenues to compete with a business major.

3. If they have an essay requirement make sure to answer the question(s) effectively. Don't spend ten minutes typing a quick answer. Treat it with the same respect you would a final paper for 50 percent of your grade. Write a first draft, re-read it, get someone else to read it, and then edit your final draft.

4. Make sure your application is mistake free.

5. Keep track of all deadlines. If a company has received 2,500 resumes for five openings, they aren't going to be inclined to really care about why you should still be able to submit your resume after the deadline. Yes, you may have found out about it late, or you were on vacation, but the fact is they probably feel confident that they can get what they need from those other 2,500 applicants who were on time.

In addition to your online search you also want to follow the companies you are most interested in on LinkedIn, Facebook, and other social media outlets. Companies will announce important internship opening and closing dates using social media. You can also read about the experiences of past interns which can provide insight into what you can expect if you are hired.

Internet Success Story

I relocated from Rochester, NY to Towson, Maryland to attend graduate school at Towson University. For two years I'd been working in college admissions at SUNY Brockport but my plans always included pursing a graduate degree. I decided that when I went back to school that I wanted to be a full-time student. My plan to be able to afford school included two parts—the first was to get a graduate assistantship and the second was to get a paid internship.

A graduate assistantship is a support position offered to graduate degree students to work at the university while in pursuit of their degree. Graduate assistantships are paid positions that can include a variety of duties from teaching, to research, to assisting athletic teams, and other roles. In exchange for their work, graduate students receive a stipend and tuition waiver. If you are considering going to graduate school, I highly encourage you to check with the institution to see how you can apply for an assistantship position. I applied for an assistantship through the Office of Graduate Studies and my resume was selected for review by the Office of Student Affairs. I was invited to interview for one of their open positions.

While I was in the process of applying for graduate assistantships, I was also looking for internships. I saw a position on monster.com for a public relations intern at a local accounting firm. I applied online and submitted my cover letter and resume. When I was called to interview for the graduate assistantship at Towson University, I coordinated my interview with the accounting firm to be the same day. I could only afford one trip to Maryland from Rochester so I had to make it count.

I interviewed for the assistantship and the public relations internship and accepted both positions. That internship introduced me to the financial industry and I got to learn about forensic accounting as I worked on email communications and the company newsletter. I moved to Maryland in May and had the chance to get acclimated to the area while working both paid roles. The internship ended for the fall and I was able to turn my attention to my classwork.

Leverage the Power of Internship Programs

Did you know that there are internship programs out there available for students that provide support, internships, and career development? When I was in college the only program I'd heard of was INROADS. I assumed that it was only for business students and failed to do my due diligence, letting the opportunity I may have had fade away. I am still pleased with the internships I was able to complete, but the benefit and value of participation in an internship program are undeniable.

Competitive internship programs are most often run by non-profit organizations and serve a role to assist students in certain populations or promote careers in a certain industry. I am not referring to internship programs ran by a company. These programs tend to require an application process to gain admission. The accepted candidates then work through the program to secure an internship with various companies or government agencies. The process is worth it considering that the majority of these programs provide paid internships, scholarships, networking opportunities, and connect you directly to companies or government agencies.

Although I did not personally obtain an internship through an internship program, I had the privilege of running one of the leading diversity internship programs in the country for five years at T. Howard Foundation. One of the biggest advantages of participating in a program is the additional support before, during, and after your internship experience. These programs are there to serve a need, provide an opportunity, and give college students the chance to have an amazing internship. Whether you are interested in business, government, communications, finance, digital media, information technology, or so many other disciplines, you can find options for programs that will fit your interest.

As I mentioned before, the support that students who participate in these types of programs receive is a major advantage. When you apply, often you leverage the power of a particular industry and are eligible for opportunities with many companies at once. With T.

Howard Foundation, students who were accepted had the opportunity to work for one of 30-40 different media or entertainment companies with one application. Also, getting connected to people and industries is key to networking. Networking is where a lot of job offers happen.

Though program participation you not only get connected to companies and the professionals you meet at your internship, but to your fellow internship program participants. While going through the program, participants are all students, but fast forward a few years and those classmates will be working professionals. Those connections can last a long time and be integral to your success.

The application process for these programs can be rigorous. Some internship programs will get hundreds of applications while others will get thousands. Depending on the program, you may or may not have to pay an application fee. Considering the wealth of opportunities available, the application fee is a minimal amount to invest if you get accepted.

Check with career services to see if they know of any programs, and beyond that perform a Google search and check with professional associations to learn if they work with or sponsor an internship program. Once you find a program that fits with your goals make sure to do your research on the program, its history, requirements, benefits, and read the alumni success stories. Ideally, you will find multiple programs to apply to and increase your chances at getting your dream internship.

Once you start the application process make sure you follow a few guidelines to make your process go smoothly.

1. Research the program to learn the history and services they provide.
2. Read the eligibility requirements to make sure you qualify for the program (GPA, class year, major, time commitments, etc.).
3. Read the application instructions and write down all deadlines so you can meet them.
4. Read and carefully follow instructions regarding any requirements for supporting materials (ex., if they say one-page resume then submit a one-page resume).
5. If they have an essay requirement make sure to answer the question(s) effectively. Don't spend 10 minutes typing a quick answer. Treat it with the same respect you would a final paper worth 50 percent of your grade. Write a first draft, re-read it, and if possible get someone else to read it, and then edit your final draft.
6. Proofread everything!
7. Practice interviewing.

Over the years I have read through thousands of applications. What never ceases to amaze me is the number of simple mistakes I come across. Proofread. Grammatical errors and misspelled words can easily be caught before submission by proofreading and editing your work. Also, if you are using the same essay for more than one program, remove the name or mention of the other program(s) from the essay.

Some student's still include an objective on their resumes (which I don't recommend). I don't recommend using an objective because it rarely every adds anything of value and it is an outdated practice. It can also lead to avoidable mistakes. I've seen a number of times where the objective states that the applicant is seeking a position with "X" company or program. Well, if I am not "X" company I am not going to give you a second look because clearly there is a lack of attention to detail displayed by not making that change.

Another mistake that students often make is failing to effectively answer the essay or short answer questions. Treat the essay as you would your interview. It is a chance to allow your voice, personality, and insights to speak for you beyond your resume, grades, and activities.

Lastly, as I have said before, do your research. Many students also make the mistake in the application and the interview of not knowing enough about the organization and the program. Failure to demonstrate your knowledge of the internship program and their mission will greatly derail your chances at gaining entry. Being unprepared for questions about the organization will reflect negatively on you. For most programs you will be competing against very strong candidates for a few openings. Getting through the application and interview process will be a great professional development experience, even if you don't land an internship.

I've included a list of internships programs. This is not an exhaustive list but a place to get you started. I encourage you to take a look at each program as the services they offer go well beyond the brief descriptions included. Although I have primarily discussed the internship advantages, these programs tend to also provide great support for participants throughout their careers from landing that first job and well beyond.

Internship Programs

Athena Collaborative: Internships for women interested in STEM (science, technology, engineering, and math) related careers, including banking and financial careers. www.athenacollaborative.org

*Hispanic Association of College and Universities (HACU) National Internship Program: Paid internships with federal government agencies and corporations. Open to all majors.

www.hacu.net/hacu/HNIP.asp

*INROADS: Paid internships with Fortune 500 companies. Open to all majors. www.inroads.org

International Radio and Television Society Foundation (IRTS) Summer Fellowship: Summer fellowship with major media companies. Paid fellowship open to all majors. www.irtsfoundation.org

Lime Connect: Exclusive resources for students with disabilities to get connected to internship opportunities (mostly paid) and career opportunities. Open to all majors. www.limeconnect.com

*Management Leadership for Tomorrow: Personalized career coaching and connections for paid internships and career opportunities for undergraduate and graduate degree seeking students from all academic majors. www.ml4t.org

*Multicultural Advertising Internship Program (MAIP): Paid internships with major advertising agencies. www.aaaa.org

*Sponsors for Educational Opportunity (SEO): Paid internships in banking and private equity, finance, technology, non-profit management, and law. Open to all majors. www.seo-usa.org

*T. Howard Foundation: Paid internships with multimedia and entertainment companies for undergraduate and graduate degree seeking students. Open to all majors. www.t-howard.org

The Washington Center Internship Program: Paid internships with non-profits, international, private sector companies, and government agencies in Washington, DC. Open to all majors. www.twc.edu

* Program targeting ethnic minority students

Five
THE INTERVIEW PROCESS

On the road to securing your internship, you will undoubtedly have an interview at some point. Being called for an interview means that your application and resume were impressive enough that the manager, hiring professional, or internship coordinator knows that you are worth speaking with. They are trying to assess if what was presented in paper matches what you will present in person.

The interview is your chance to get beyond the black and white of a resume and share with a company why you are the best candidate. Interviews also serve as an opportunity for you to learn more about the company and their expectations for their interns. The interview is the make or break point. You want to approach your interview as well prepared as possible. Remember when I talked about the internship being the "icing on the cake" to your education and the interview being the "taste test?" This is the final test, the opportunity to put your best foot forward and seal the deal.

Having done a lot of internships means that I've been on a lot of internship interviews. In addition to that, I held part-time jobs while in college and graduate school. Professionally I've held several positions, bringing my personal total to well over 25 interviews that I've had to go through (many positions required multiple interviews). I understand very well what it is like to sit in that interview chair, trying your best to demonstrate that you are the best candidate to all they desire in an intern.

Even with that experience, I will be talking to you

The most common feedback I get from hiring managers and human resources professionals is, "The candidate was unprepared and knew nothing about us or the position."

---

mainly from my experiences as the interviewer. Working in college admissions I did admissions interviews (almost every day) for nearly a decade. When I was with the T. Howard program, my staff and I conducted approximately 500 interviews (Skype, phone, and in-person) over a four-month period (October – January) every year of students seeking to get into the program. I personally conducted about 100-200 interviews per cycle. While my advice might not be scientific, it is coming from years spent as the interviewer and the interviewee.

Interview Preparation

Preparation is key. All too often candidates for internships and jobs go into their interviews unprepared. The most common feedback I get from hiring managers and human resources professionals is, "The candidate was unprepared and knew nothing about us or the position." The saddest part is that it is easily avoidable. It takes a little time, energy, and effort to properly prepare for the interview. It is time well spent when you can stand out from amongst the crowd by just showing that you've done your homework. Being knowledgeable about the company and your potential role demonstrates that you are serious about the position, have a sincere interest in who they are and what they do, and that you are a self-starter.

So, how can you walk into an interview and show that you have done your homework? It starts with a little bit of research. You should have already conducted some research on the company before you applied and know something about it. If you applied without doing any research, you definitely need to get on the ball. You can search using the following resources:

Company website. The company website will give you the basic run down on the company's history, mission, and values. Visit the About Us page to find out more about the company. You should also gather information on the company size and locations. For smaller companies, this might be your only resource for gathering information.

News. Larger companies will have a section on their website dedicated to news and press releases. This is a great spot to see what has been going on at the company in terms of major shakeups at the top, new products, research, community events, or new locations.

Investor Relations. Major companies use this section to communicate with shareholders and explain the financial status of the company. You can also often find the annual report for a company, which tends to give details about the direction of the company for the near future.

Social Media Accounts. Follow the company on LinkedIn, investigate their Facebook page, check out the images they are posting on Instagram, and observe the tone of their tweets on Twitter. Diving into their social media presence can give you a sense of the product, brand, and personality they use to communicate with their audience and attract new customers. Is the company very active, engaging, and informal on social media, or is it a company that just uses social media to deliver news?

Company review sites. Glassdoor.com is the most popular among websites that allow users to read reviews of companies. Current and former employees as well as interns provide anonymous reviews and ratings of companies they've worked for.

Your own network. You may have a classmate and friend who has worked at a company that you are trying to get an internship with. Ask around and also see if you are connected to anyone through your LinkedIn profile that you can have a chat with about the internship program or company overall.

Search engines. Whether it's Google, Bing, or Yahoo, go to your search engine of choice to do your research. Be careful not to become so engaged with stories and sites that might be less than credible. Rather, use a search engine to locate competitors in the industry and to see what is happening in the industry overall. Trade publications and their websites are good for understanding the state of the industry you are interested in as well.

Of course, you won't remember everything you see online which is why you should be taking notes. The things that you want to be more certain about will be the basics, including company mission, value, and leadership. If you want to impress your interviewer, being able to form a question based on your extensive research is one way to do so. For example, you may have found out in the annual report that they are launching a new product later in the year. You could ask a question such as this:

"I recently read that the company is launching a new XYZ later this year. That seems like a very exciting venture. What role if any do you anticipate this department having in that launch?"

Even if the department is not directly involved in that product launch, you would have shown that you know and care what is happening with the company. You should have three to five thoughtful questions to ask after they are done questioning you. Don't give a great interview only to end with a whimper and not ask a single question. Finish strong, and while you are asking your questions, stay confident.

Here are a few questions to get you thinking. You should of course build your list of questions after you've done your research:

1. What are some of the upcoming projects that I will get to work on?
2. What led you to choose a career with this company?
3. When you think back to your most outstanding intern, what made him/her such a great asset?
4. How many people would I be working with and reporting to?
5. What are the next steps in this process?

Make sure you have read the internship job description for the role you are interviewing for. Also, if they have an internship website, read that forward and backwards to get a sense of the internship program and what interns get to work on. Some companies have very robust internship programs that will include activities like lunches with executives and company outings. If you know who will be doing the interview you can even try and learn things about their professional background through LinkedIn.

All of your research is meant to help you be prepared to artfully articulate what you know about the company and how you can fit their needs. Knowing the mission statement and what the company sales were the previous year are great but being able to incorporate that type of information into your answers is where you begin to separate yourself from the pack.

Having a Successful Interview

When you say "job interview" the image that may come to mind is similar to a scene in a movie. You might picture a big executive office with a huge, expensive, wooden desk and a stuffy corporate executive on the other side of it. Today's job interview landscape has changed as technology has produced free and low cost video conferencing software and organizations have become more flexible. How and where companies conduct interviews is changing.

Yes, many interviews will still take place in an office behind an intimidating desk or table, but increasingly companies are conducting interviews via Skype, Oovoo, or iChat, and at locations like Starbucks, Panera Bread, or over dinner. With more relaxed venue or scenery, it is tempting to become more relaxed yourself and perhaps not take the interview with the right attitude. No matter if your interview is done virtually or in an office, you want to convey the right attitude and maintain your professionalism.

Make the time to practice, practice, practice. The best way to simulate an interview is to schedule a mock interview with your career services office. This will allow you to go through the steps of dressing professionally, showing up on time, and being in the "hot seat" of getting questions asked of you. A mock interview will help you learn how to be quick on your feet, answer behavioral questions that might otherwise throw you off, and learn how to share your story.

During your mock interview, you will be provided with an assessment from your interviewer that will make you aware of things you might not have noticed, such as the nervous energy of tapping your foot, or if your appearance was not professional enough. It is better to find that out now than wonder why no one is calling you back. If your interview will be over the phone or video service, then request that your mock interview be completed using that method to get comfortable with trying to connect to an audience virtually.

If you have the option to have your session recorded, then you should do so. In watching yourself on camera you will notice your body language as well as how clearly you speak and how well you maintain eye contact. In the event you can't participate in a mock interview through career services, you can ask a professor, mentor, or search online for a career coach that offers that service. There are various types of interview formats that you might find yourself needing to prepare for.

Types of Interviews
- Phone
- Video
- One-on-One
- Panel

Phone Interviews

Very often a phone interview/phone screen will be the first interview that you go through. A phone screen interview is generally conducted by a recruiter, internship coordinator, or a hiring manager. Initial phone screens are relatively brief, lasting 10-20 minutes. Usually this conversation determines if the candidate is good enough to move forward in the process. If the company is not very large and you are not local, your phone interview could be the only interview.

Based on your location, your second interview could also be conducted via telephone. The second interview will be longer and more in-depth. It is super important that you prepare properly for a phone interview with the same level of attention as an in-person interview.

Video Interviews

In the last few years, video interviews using Skype or other similar services have grown more popular. It is a great way for a company to interview a candidate but still make a visual connection. Companies are opting for these interviews also because it is cheaper than flying candidates in. Video interviews, like phone interviews, should be taken with the same level of seriousness as if being conducted in person.

To have a successful video or phone interview you should do the following:

Dress professionally

Phone: Although it might seem like overkill, you should dress professionally even though your interviewers can't see you. This might sound strange, but it works. The psychology behind this suggestion is that as a result of dressing professionally, your attitude will reflect it. Your posture, your professionalism, word choice, and even confidence can be influenced by what you wear.

Video: Obviously, during a video interview your interviewers can see you so you should dress appropriately. You might be thinking, well they can only see a part of me from about the chest up, so why would I dress in a complete outfit? Well, what if for some reason you did have to get up and when you did it revealed that you were wearing sweat pants? Don't assume that it can't happen.

Get to a quiet place

Phone: To avoid distractions and to make it as easy as possible for the interviewer to hear you, conduct your interview in a quiet place. Don't try and do your interview in the hall between classes or while riding the bus. If your parked car is the only quiet place you can find then that is an option, but not while driving. You should be in a stable, quiet place where you have a strong signal and you can focus and concentrate.

If you have roommates, let them know that you are going to be on an interview and ask them to keep noise to a minimum for that short period of time. Put the pets outside or into another room. You should be prepared with a copy of your resume, your research notes, pen, and paper.

Video: You want to avoid distractions in the background. Make sure the place where you have the camera set up doesn't display distracting posters and has good lighting. Don't conduct interviews from your bed or while walking using your camera phone. Again, leave the pets outside and let others know that you will be doing an interview so that you don't get "photo bombed" in the middle of a question. Also close all other programs on your computer. Getting Facebook, email, or IM notifications during an interview is distracting to you and your interviewer. Turn your cell phone off.

Very often career services centers will have interview rooms that you can use. Make sure you can get cell phone reception and/or Wi-Fi. Sometimes they can supply you with a web camera or a landline if needed. If you need assistance, just ask.

Smile

Phone: Even though they can't see you smile during your phone interview, smiling will make you sound more energetic and engaged. Since they can't see you, smiling becomes very important as a way to try and convey some of your pleasant personality.

Video: In a video, they can of course see your smile, movements, and body language. It is important to sit up straight, look into the camera (not at the screen), and try to connect with your interviewers.

Use a landline or make sure you are in a good service area

Phone: If you still have a landline phone, use it. There won't be any dropped calls or static. If you don't have a landline, make sure you are in a strong service area where your call won't drop. It is best for you to be stationary. I recommend disabling your call waiting, but if that is not possible, just don't answer the beep if you get another call.

Video: Having a good, strong signal is important in a video interview as well. Slow signals lead to buffering, delays, and unstable video feeds. You get annoyed when talking to a friend and that happens, so imagine the annoyance on the side of the interviewer. Test your connection within the software or by reaching out to a friend.

Do not eat or chew gum

Eating and chewing gum is rude, and you wouldn't do it in an in-person interview. If you scheduled your interview around lunchtime, grab a snack before the interview or just wait until it is over.

Have a professional profile image

Your video service profile photo should be professional. If you are using Skype and have a photo linked to your account, make sure it is a professional one. That is the first image the interviewer will see. Also, much like your email address, make sure your Skype username is one that is professional in nature as well. You can always create a separate account to use for interviews.

One-on-One and Panel Interviews

Interviews are more commonly taking place in bars, coffee shops, restaurants, and hotel lobbies but many will still be at the company in an office. Be prepared in case you walk into a room and discover multiple people in the interview. Panel interviews may consist of different representatives from various departments that interact with the role, or it could be just members of the department that you would be interning in. The trickiest part about a panel interview can be figuring out who to look at and trying to connect with multiple people. I've been on both sides of the process. When conducting panel interviews, it has always been off-putting when the interviewee doesn't make eye contact with everyone, especially the person asking them a question. You don't want to stare any one person in the room down, but you do what to acknowledge the presence of all parties.

If there is a person who you deem to be of more importance (i.e., president of the company, etc.) in the room, don't minimize the others around the table by not making eye contact or asking them questions when the time comes. A good leader is going to appreciate that you treated everyone respectfully. No matter the setting, the same concepts apply. This is your chance to put your best foot forward.

Dress professionally

You've heard it said before, but what is professional dress? Refer to the Dress for Success section at the end of this chapter for tips on professional attire for men and women. Also bring copies of your resume, a notepad, and pen. Now would be a good time to invest in a nice portfolio case to carry those items.

Scout out your commute

Take the time to research the location and figure out how you will get there, where to park, the closest public transportation, exact fare, etc. You don't want to discover on the morning of your interview that the new construction project has blocked the street or that it is a 30-minute walk from the nearest bus or train station. Often the interviewer will provide instructions on getting to their office. If they do, you still want to make sure you understand them before you head out the door.

Be on time

It is better to arrive to the general area early than to be late. You don't want to walk into the office 45 minutes before the interview either, though. If you arrive very early, pop into a local coffee shop for a few minutes so that you can gather your thoughts and read your notes. If the building has a lobby, you could sit there for a few minutes, or if you drove, once you find a parking spot, take a few moments before going in. If your interview is scheduled for 1:00 p.m. then by 12:45 p.m. you should be reaching the office to announce to the receptionist that you have arrived.

Make eye contact and watch your body language

When you walk into the room, do so confidently. Make eye contact and extend your hand for a firm handshake. Not comfortable? Then grab a friend or mentor and practice making a firm introduction until it feels natural. If there is a panel of interviewers, make sure to greet everyone and shake their hands. Once you are instructed to take a seat, sit up straight, be attentive, and don't forget to breathe!

Follow their lead on ordering food

The idea of having an interview over food can seem like a good or bad thing. It doesn't have to be overwhelming. To make it easy on yourself, follow the lead of the interviewer. If they order a salad, you shouldn't look for the most expensive item on the menu. Try to stay in the same ballpark as far as price goes. Consider too that eating a salad or simple entrée might be more manageable then trying to answer questions in between bites of a messy burger or with chicken wing juice dripping down your hands. The focus is not on the meal; your focus needs to be on performing well at your interview.

If you are just having coffee then go with something that won't give you coffee breath. Water is always safe. If you are of legal drinking age, even if you see your interviewer order alcohol, don't do it. There will be plenty of time to celebrate once you get the position.

Follow Up

No matter the type of interview you have, it is very important to follow up with a thank you note to the interviewer(s), reiterating your interest in the position. It can be done via email or you can go the route of mailing a handwritten thank you card. You can purchase a stack of thank you cards from your local office supply store or even your university bookstore. Your thank you note or email does not have to be very long so don't turn it into a complete book. Keep it brief. You should send your letters out within 48 hours of the interview.

In today's current hiring environment, even for internships, it is common for candidates to go through multiple rounds of interviews. If you find yourself in that position, you should follow up with a thank you letter after each interview, as it is likely to be with different people. To follow up your panel interview, you can write one letter in care of the contact person who scheduled the interview, but make sure to address it to the *Selection Committee,* or you can send each member of the committee a personal email or letter.

Dress for Success

Arriving at your interview wearing the wrong clothes will get the interview off on the wrong foot before you even take a seat. It isn't difficult to find professional clothes at a reasonable price. You don't have to go to a high-end retailer if you don't have the money. Stores like Macy's, H&M, Target, Marshalls, or even Burlington Coat Factory can offer you a variety of prices and selection. Thrift shops can also produce great cost effective finds. You will want to start building your wardrobe with professional clothes sooner rather than later so that when you do get that professional internship, you will have clothes to wear to work. To complete your professional appearance, carry copies of your resume, a notepad, and pen in a nice business portfolio or attaché case. It is time to ditch the book bag.

Professional Attire

Men
- Ironed long-sleeve button down shirt (white or coordinated with suit)
- Suit (solid color - black, grey, dark blue, or brown)
- Belt (should match your shoes)
- Neck tie (avoid loud colors and flashy ties)
- Dark socks
- Polished dress shoes
- Little to no jewelry (removing earrings is safest)
- Go easy on the after shave or avoid it all together
- Neatly trimmed and clean nails
- Neatly trimmed facial hair
- Get a haircut
- Portfolio or briefcase (no book bags)

Women
- Suit – Pants or Skirt (solid color - black, grey, dark blue, or brown). The skirt should be long to cover your thighs when seated

- Coordinated blouse
- Conservative shoes (closed toed pumps, no extremes in height)
- Limited jewelry (think small earrings, watch, and a ring or two at most)
- Professional hairstyle
- Neutral pantyhose
- Light make-up
- Avoid perfume
- Neatly manicured clean nails (avoid loud colors of nail polish)
- Portfolio or briefcase (no book bags)

Everyone
- Make sure your clothes are pressed.
- Make sure your clothes fit appropriately, not too small or large.
- Remove tags from new clothes.
- Turn off your cell phone.
- Take off your headphones.
- Remove your sun glasses.
- Consider removing body piercings (lips, nose, chin, check, and eyebrow).
- Cover your tattoos.

Covering up tattoos and removing body piercings is the most common practice for those trying to land internships in corporate settings. You have no idea if the person (or people) conducting your interview will be very conservative or covered in tattoos themselves. Do not give the interviewers the chance to potentially be distracted or make assumptions about you based on appearance, so removing them is the best option.

Be aware, however, that you should investigate company policy surrounding body art and piercings. Some companies have policies about the length of your hair exceeding your shirt collar if you are a male. Some policies for women may require that pantyhose be worn with dresses or skirts. These are all realities of working in professional environments. For 8-12 weeks of an internship it is bearable. Later in your career you want to investigate policies that may dissuade you from working in certain environments before you accept a job.

One more word of caution on something that I've observed during student interviews—the tendency to get too comfortable. When an interview is going well, you must resist the urge to drop your level of professionalism. Even if your interviewer appears to be only a few years older than you, don't assume that you can slip into using slang or colloquialisms. I am not saying that you should sound robotic or not let your personality shine through, but you do want to remain professional for the duration of the interview.

The last search you should perform online is for

popular interview questions. Work towards increasing your knowledge of how to answer some of those questions. Take advantage of practicing your answers but avoid sounding too rehearsed or robotic. Some interviews you will knock out of the park, others you will do okay, and some just won't be that good. It's okay. With each experience you will get better at this process.

Six

PAID VS UNPAID INTERNSHIPS

In recent years there has been much controversy surrounding unpaid internships. There have been lawsuits brought by former interns against companies with claims that their duties were not those of interns but those of employees, and that by virtue of the types of work they completed, they should be compensated. You can search online to learn the more intricate details surrounding various lawsuits.

My aim is not to delve into the details and legalities of paid versus unpaid internship but to deal more with the challenge not receiving compensation presents for some financially. The dilemma that many students face is the desire to do an internship versus the need to save money for tuition and living expenses. This is a very valid concern. Of my eight internships, four of them were not paid.

Two of my unpaid internships occurred over different summers—my sales and marketing internship with the Rochester Red Wings baseball team and the public relations internship with the Sojourner House. Those summers were especially busy for me. In order to do those internships I had to work part-time jobs at the same time.

During my internship with the Rochester Red Wings, I started in mid-spring semester. Over the semester, I worked 20 hours per week, carried 15 credits, and worked a part-time job at a movie theater. When the semester ended, I worked 40 hours per week

---

Ultimately, on your resume, the potential employer won't know if the internship experience was for academic credit or not, or if it was paid or not. What they will know is that you have some skills that you've earned that might just solve a need that they have.

---

briefly at my internship. After a few weeks, I asked my manager if I could cut my hours to only work on game days. I made that adjustment so that I could work more hours at the movie theatre. I wanted the experience but I had tuition to pay that coming fall, so I made it work. While I interned at Sojourner House, the non-profit, I worked at the movie theatre and as a part-time receptionist at a hospital in the evenings. I pretty much spent my summers at work, all of the time.

I completed an unpaid internship during the fall of my senior year with the communications department at SUNY Oswego. I worked with the department chair to create brochures and marketing materials to advertise the newly approved degree in public relations. When I started the program, the college offered a Bachelor's degree in Communications with a Public Relations track. Moving to offer a Bachelors of Arts in Public Relations was going to attract new students who were looking for that specific degree. I was excited to be able to assist the department in spreading the word. Since I did not have to be in an office to complete that internship, it gave me a lot of flexibility.

While completing the unpaid internship with the communications department, I was also doing my paid internship with Enterprise Rent-A-Car. It was a very busy schedule but I made it work. I had to have exceptional time management skills to keep up with my responsibilities, perform above average at my internship, maintain my grades, and hold the office of president of a campus organization. The key to keeping it together is to stay organized and stay focused. When you are at one place, give that job or internship your full attention.

In the spring of my senior year, rather than taking it easy before graduation, I did an unpaid internship with the New York State Power Authority for two days a week while I continued my internship with Enterprise Rent-A-Car. On top of that I was still working at my paid internship in SUNY Oswego's public affairs office.

Yes, I worked hard and I worked a lot, but I still had a life, hung out with friends, and went to parties and events. There were times I had to make sacrifices, but for the most part, I was a normal college student—but with less free time. I had to keep organized in order to not let things spiral out of control. As a senior, I had a good sense of what I could handle academically and socially while working and interning. As a freshman, you don't want to overload yourself too soon while you are making the adjustment from high school to college. If you are strategic about your plans, you can fit an unpaid internship into your schedule and still work a paid job elsewhere, without letting your grades suffer.

Another option to consider is doing your internship for academic credit. I only completed two of my internships for academic credit. My time with the New York Power Authority James Fitzpatrick Power Plant and my internship with my school's communications department were both for academic credit. Check with your school's career services office because your school may have specific requirements for what they can count as an internship. Also, check with your academic major department. It is becoming more common that schools are requiring internships to graduate, and you want to make sure you are in compliance.

Both of my internships for academic credit were completed during the academic semester. I elected to not participate in internships for academic credit over the summer because at my school, it would have required me to pay tuition for the credit hours. Paying for the credit hours over the summer would have reduced the amount of money I had available to pay for school in the fall and spring.

Some companies require that you receive academic credit for participating in their internship program. You will have to investigate this requirement with each company and make the best decision for your situation. Ultimately, on your resume, the potential employer won't know if the internship experience was for academic credit or not, or if it was paid or not. What they will know is that you have some skills that you've earned that might just solve a need that they have.

Educational Value

In terms of the functional differences of participating in a paid versus unpaid internship, there will most likely be many. If a company hasn't invested money developing a paid internship program, they probably don't have a formalized program. A formalized internship program will require evaluation on the part of the company to ensure that the goals of the program are being met. Formal programs tend to come with greater accountability on the side of the company. If the company program has organizational goals to meet, they will work harder to create more challenging and fulfilling learning experiences for their interns.

An unpaid internship with no formal internship program will often lack structure to ensure that interns are able to have a valuable learning experience. In my own internships, while unpaid, the Rochester Red Wings and the New York Power Authority had structured programs that outlined the internship expectations and measured success. At the non-profit internship, with no formal programs, things were a bit freer flowing. I often had to suggest activities that I could do that would be new or allow me to apply skills I'd learned in the classroom.

For new or first time interns, you should not be as worried about a paid versus unpaid internship, but more concerned if the company has a structured program. If you have done multiple internships, having an internship experience that is a little more self-directed can allow for more flexibility to try things that might not be available in more formal programs. For example, if you were interning for a small store as a social media intern to build their social media presence, it is likely that you would have great latitude in creating a strategy and you would be seen as the expert. You wouldn't have the guidance that a formal program or the oversight. That could be good or bad based on your level of ability and your desire to be taught by others rather than being the authority.

When I spoke with one of my former interns, Olivia Grant, about her experience, she offered an interesting perspective. As a Visual Culture and Psychology major at Wesleyan University, she completed five internships, paid and unpaid, at smaller companies and major companies like Edelman, AMC Networks, and Viacom. She presently works for Viacom–BET Networks in Programming and Acquisitions.

"I think college students should participate in at least one internship (although I think at least three) because it's crucial to have experience under your belt. It's necessary to learn how to be professional and how to communicate with clients, managers, bosses, and coworkers. One also has the chance to make connections in their chosen industry because that's how you find out about a lot of opportunities.

With that said, it's important for college students to shoot for an internship that pays or at least has a formal internship program. Paid internships typically introduce interns to a variety of departments and people in the company. They should also be able to work on an independent project so they have something to show for their time at the internship. They need to build a portfolio of work and results before graduating because it's a competitive world out there!

People in paid internships tend to fare better in the long run because companies are investing money teaching college students about their company and their industry with the hope of cultivating talent for their organization in the future," says Olivia.

Some people balk automatically at the idea of working for free and steer clear of what they would consider to be "free labor." While I can understand how participating in an unpaid internship can be a struggle when you need money, be creative and you can get an experience while not jeopardizing your financial goals. If money is a concern, intern part-time and work part-time. You can also look for telecommuting internships in areas like graphic design, social media, or writing.

Seven

GET OUT OF THE COMFORT ZONE: INTERNING AWAY FROM HOME

After you decide that you want to do an internship, a big part of your plan will be deciding where you want to intern. The where is not just in regards to the name of a company, but the location of your internship across the United States or even the world. Every summer, interns pack up and hit the road to participate in summer internships in many of the major cities in the U.S. Some of the more popular destinations include Los Angeles, New York, Washington, DC, Chicago, and Atlanta. Don't be intimidated or cut yourself off from opportunities in different cities and even different parts of the world. Explore the possibility to see if you can make it happen.

Start planning early and gathering the costs of housing, transportation, and other considerations to intern away from home. There are probably great internship opportunities in your own backyard, too, but if you want to spend the summer on Wall Street... well there is only one Wall Street. Getting a jump on the process gives you more planning time and savings time.

Yet again, doing your research is going to be key to success in landing a gig away from home. Looking back on that internship goal you set initially, will you be able to achieve that goal staying in your neck of the woods? Are you set on interning with a major sports team, or

---

Don't be intimidated or cut yourself off from opportunities in different cities and even different parts of the world. Explore the possibility to see if you can make it happen.

---

working for a specific company, or have your eye on a certain industry? Those factors will drive your internship search and assist you in determining if you have to be in a major city. The other truth is that while you can do a social media internship almost anywhere, you might just *want* to spend the summer amidst the hustle and bustle of New York or another city. Whether it is a need or a want to be in a major city, if you have determined that you are not going to be near your home for your internship, you have to have a plan and strategy in place to make it happen.

Picking a City

If you are open to all of the possibilities that exist, you will really need to focus. Trying to conduct a broad search of every internship, in every major city, is not going to get you anywhere. When I was recruiting students for a national internship program, students would often tell me, "I'll go anywhere I can get an internship." Well, it isn't always that simple. While I can appreciate the willingness to take advantage of any opportunity to be adventurous, the process of relocating for a summer is not so simplistic.

The majority of companies do not provide internship housing. You will most likely be responsible for finding a place to live, paying for it, and providing your own transportation. When you factor that into the equation, it would be a difficult task to try and research housing in ten different cities on top of your internship search. You can narrow your city selection down by one of these three ways:

1. Select a few target companies that might be located all in one city.

2. Select an industry (ex., if you want to work in federal government, Washington, DC would be a likely choice).
3. Select a city that you have friends or family in for housing, and then look for internships that meet your goals.

If you have chosen to apply to an internship program similar to those I mentioned in the previous chapter, then you will have more support in the relocation process. They will be able to guide you towards resources for housing, but you will still need to do much of the work yourself. Your choices of city will be based on where that particular internship program offers opportunities.

The other resource that can assist you with your quest to do an internship in a major city will be your school. Some schools, including Syracuse University, SUNY Oswego, Emerson College, University of Texas at Austin, and James Madison University offer students the opportunity to intern or have an experiential learning experience in Los Angeles. Start with your career services office, office of experiential learning, or academic department to find out if your school participates. Those programs can vary from a few weeks to an entire semester. The costs will range widely; however, you may be able to use your financial aid towards your expenses.

Start With Your Network

How do you find temporary housing in a city halfway across the country from where you live? Start by reaching out to your family, friends, and your extended network. If you will require the support of your parents you should discuss your interest in interning away from home with them early in the process. If they are in support of your decision, they may assist you financially if your internship doesn't pay enough to afford rent. Also, you don't want to accept an internship only to find out later that your parents don't approve of your decision to relocate. You know best the type of relationship you have with your parents and what does and does not need to be discussed.

Checking with your family is also good because you may find out about other factors that could interfere with your internship plans. Extended family vacations, weddings, or other special events could occur that you might not be able to participate in if you are away. There are some students with family obligations (working to provide support, caring for a sibling or parent, etc.) that may prevent them from taking advantage of going away. If you are in that situation, don't get discouraged but take advantage of internships closer to home. You can still have an incredible experience and financially if your internship is paid you will come out ahead.

Family is also a good place to start because they might be aware of family members or friends living in the city that you want to be in. Knowing someone who lives in that city could potentially mean a place to stay or at least a person local to the area who can assist you in finding a place to stay. You never know all of the connections and resources of another person.

Moving beyond your family, you should think of friends and extended networks of people that you know. Are you a member of a fraternity or sorority, a professional student association, a national volunteer organization, or a religious organization? Does your college have an alumni network that connects current students with alumni in other areas? Use the resources around you to get moving on finding housing. Professional organizations sometimes offer scholarships for members. Those scholarship dollars could solve your relocation money problems.

Check with your academic department, academic advisor, or career services about housing assistance. There are sometimes grant funds available to assist students interested in participating in internships. If you've gone through this process and have at least started your research, when you do get a call for an interview in a different city, you will feel much more comfortable if the question of housing comes up.

Where to Stay

For interns seeking summer housing in NY, LA, and DC, on campus housing at local colleges and universities are a great option for students to consider. By living on campus you will be close to public transportation, campus security, and have options for a meal plan, and you won't have to worry about furniture. For many parents, knowing that their son or daughter is staying on a college campus gives them a level of comfort. New York and Washington, DC offer the most options for residence hall campus living for summer interns.

At T. Howard Foundation, I often walked students through the process of selecting university housing options in NY, LA, and DC. Starting in early January of the year you want to intern, you should visit the websites for the colleges you are interested in living. Most common information will be housed on the Residential life webpage. You will find the application, the expected fees, and the process are generally available online. Be prepared to submit a deposit with your application.

Residence halls will typically give you the choice of a single, double, triple, or a quad room. A single room will be the most expensive while a quad (four-person room) will be the most affordable option. Although living on a college campus has huge benefits from safety to meal plans to making it easier to meet people in a city you don't know, it can get costly. The type of room you choose and the length of your stay will impact your financial bottom line. Expect to pay somewhere between $1,000 to $3,500 or more for the summer. Similar to living on campus at your school (if you do), the bill must be paid before you move in so you can't necessarily expect to pay for housing from your internship paycheck.

University Housing

<u>NY:</u> New York University, Columbia University, The New School, The Kings College, and Fashion Institute of Design and Technology

<u>LA:</u> Summer Housing: University of California Los Angeles (UCLA)

<u>DC:</u> American University, George Mason University, Catholic University, George Washington University, Georgetown University

Other housing options include:
Family or friends
Airbnb or furnapt.com
UCLA – ucla.uloop.com

Student sublets
Corporate Rentals
Oakwood Temporary Housing – National
National Corporate Housing – National
Churchill Corporate Housing - National
Educational Housing Services – New York
Zuma Housing – Los Angeles
Solutions in LA – Los Angeles
Park Le Brea Apartments – Los Angeles

Corporate housing at places such as Oakwood Temporary Housing or Park Le Brea offer single rooms or options for roommates as well. Apartments are a popular option in Los Angeles as there are fewer colleges that open their doors to non-students. The units are fully furnished and often offer other amenities such as a gym or pool. Corporate housing can get quite costly at a few thousand dollars per month. I've assisted students in finding summer housing using Airbnb with no issues. They provide protections for all parties in the transaction that can make the renter and landlord feel more comfortable. You can of course ask friends, family, and search online for additional housing options.

How to Find Housing

Work through these housing related questions and you will find that when you start the search process things will fall into place much easier. Using this list will keep you from forgetting small details about your stay, your costs, and your commute. Don't overlook them or simply assume you won't have an issue. Try to have a viable solution for each issue and you will feel better, and if they are involved, so will your parents.

Housing/Food: Where do I plan to stay, and how will I eat?

General
o   After accepting an internship, how long will I have to find housing?
o   Will the internship company help me find housing, or do I have to do it on my own?
o   Will I need housing for more than 10 weeks?
o   When am I expected to arrive, and when is the last day of my internship?
o   What is my monthly budget for housing, food, and transportation?
o   How far is the closest grocery store to where I plan to live? Are there restaurants or affordable options for eating nearby if I won't have a car (in LA or DC)?

University
o How much will it cost for a single, double, triple, or quad room?
o How much is the application fee and deposit, and when will they be due?
o Is a meal plan offered and if so, how much will it cost?
o If I don't take the meal plan, are there food options available close by?
o Will I have access to on campus facilities such as the gym, computer lab, and library?
o If I bring a car, will I have to pay for parking?
o How much do the laundry facilities cost?

Sublet, Corporate Rentals, and Hostels
o How much is the average rent in the area?
o Do I need to sublet a place located near food and public transportation?
o If I am under 18, will I need a parent to sign the lease for me?
o Will I have a roommate I don't know?
o Am I looking for an apartment for myself, or a bedroom in an apartment or house?
o Is it near a laundry facilities, or is there laundry on-site?

Family/Friends

o How far does my relative live from the internship? Large metropolitan areas can cover a lot of territory so do not assume that your commute will be brief.

o Make sure your friend/family member's house will be available for the dates you need.

o Ask where you will be sleeping. You may be under the impression that they have an extra room for you but you could arrive and be directed to a not so comfy couch. There is nothing wrong with sleeping on a couch or air mattress; however, if you were expecting a private guest bedroom that could create an uncomfortable situation.

o Will you be expected to pay rent? Don't assume it is free.

o Do they have parking (if you will have a car)?

o Will you need to purchase your own groceries?

o Are there any restrictions to how late you can come in (will they have an issue with you coming in very late from a night on the town)?

o Are there other people you will encounter who live or stay there frequently (ex., boyfriends, girlfriends, etc.)?

Transportation

o How am I going to get to work every day?

o If I will be taking public transportation, how much will it cost?

- In New York, public transportation is reliable and frequent while in Los Angeles, you could be met with challenges.
- How long of a commute is acceptable for me?
- How am I going to get to my internship city? Plane, train, bus, or car?
- Am I going to ship my personal belongings or take only what I can fit into a few bags?
- How am I going to get back home when the internship is over?
- Do I need to ask my parents' permission to take my car?
- If I am driving very far, do I have someone who is willing to ride with me?
- How much will it cost to ship my car rather than drive?
- Where will I park my car, and will it cost me money?
- If I do not have a car, how close will I be to food and entertainment?

Money
- What is my budget? How much will I earn weekly at my internship? You should create a budget that not only includes your rent but also utilities, commute, food, entertainment, cell phone, gas, and other regular expenses you have now.

o Budget forms are available online through websites like, goodfinancialcents.com, suzeorman.com, everydollar.com, or mint.com.
o How much does the internship pay?
o How often will I get paid?
o If I can't afford to pay my rent with my internship salary, where will I get more money?

Resist the urge to take on debt to complete an internship. There will be opportunities closer to home that may not require taking on debt. Using a credit card or loan for this purpose may seem like a good idea right now, but when you start to think about your student loan payments (if you have any), adding credit card debt to that won't feel good later. Eight internships and successful career later, I never interned away from home and still had ample opportunity to build my resume. If you are not a senior, and interning in another city is a goal, you now know what to do to make it happen before you graduate.

Eight
BECOMING THE
EXCEPTIONAL INTERN

Congratulations on getting your internship. If you haven't yet, I believe, and you must believe, that you will soon. Now, how do you go about being the perfect intern? After you officially accept the position, go celebrate your accomplishment. Moving forward, you should communicate with the contact person at your new internship about your start date, end date, salary, and what type of information you will need to bring with you on your first day. They will most likely provide you with similar information that you had for your interview in terms of directions to the office, where to park, and those types of logistics.

If you are interning out of town, make sure to coordinate your transportation and move in dates to allow for time to arrive one to two days before your start date. Scheduling your arrival a few days in advance also lets you make a test run to your new job so you can find the best commute. At the end of your internship, give yourself another one to two days to move out. Moving out of your housing on the last day of your internship is going to cause added stress and headaches. On your last day, you want to worry only about finishing strong and making sure you have secured recommendations and contacts for the future.

During your communications with your contact, you should ask about the office dress code. The office or department you work in could be a business casual

---

Remain teachable. No one of us is perfect so there will be a time when you get feedback that you did something wrong. When you get feedback on a project, do not take it to heart as criticism but as a learning opportunity. Ask questions so that you can learn how you can be better at the next opportunity.

---

work environment or they could require professional business dress. Business casual is a little more relaxed and will generally allow for men to wear khakis, Dockers, or dress pants, and not require a suit and tie, whereas professional dress would require a suit and tie. For women, professional dress would also be a suit and business casual would be no suit. Business casual does not, however, mean that you can wear jeans, open toed shoes, or sneakers. Whatever the policy, clarify it with the human resources department or your manager prior to your first day if you are unsure.

Make an attempt to include all of your questions in one email or phone call. The person you are communicating with has other interns, employees, and other work related demands. Answering several emails from you could get to bit overwhelming. If they provide you with a welcome email or packet, make sure to read that first as many questions might be answered within that content.

Day One

Just like you did for the interview, be on time (which is really 15 minutes early). Lay out your clothes the evening before so you don't have to waste any time in the morning. Make sure you know how to get there, where to report, and who to report too, especially if your internship is not at the same place you had your interview. Remember to bring your driver's license or non-driver's ID card and social security card or passport. Most of the time those items will be required to get a company ID and to get paid.

You may find that your first day is filled with tours of the building and office, introductions to staff members, human resources paperwork, and lunch. Take notes and be sure to greet each person with a smile and firm handshake. Take your smile to work from the second you get off the train or out of the car. You never know who you will meet in the parking lot, hallway, walking into the building, or on the elevator. Make sure you understand who's who in the office, who you report to, and who they report to.

You should also try to meet your fellow interns as you could end up working on projects together. Many companies will have an intern orientation for all interns within the first few days. These are overall introductions to the company and also allow you to meet other interns from other departments.

On your first day, I recommend sending a brief introductory email to the folks in your department. Tell them who you are, where you go to school, your major, and what you will be doing as an intern (if you know). Check with your immediate supervisor *first* to see if this is okay. An email may have already been sent out to everyone about you joining the team before you arrived.

Sample Email

Hello Everyone,

I am Sharise Kent and I will be interning here in the Communications department this summer. I am a rising senior at XXX University where I am majoring in English. I am thrilled to be a part of your team for the next few months. I look forward to working with you as well as learning from each of you.

Sincerely,
Sharise Kent
Communications Intern

Each office is different and each manager is different. Some managers will do an excellent job of taking you around and introducing you to the team, they may have refreshments on your first morning, or even take you to lunch. Some places, your manger might greet you, show you to your desk, and put you to work. It is hard to say what situation you will be walking into. Even if you are not taken around to each person, make it your priority over your first few days to introduce yourself to each person in your office.

Day Two and Beyond

There are a few simple things that you can do to stand out from your peers. We've established that dressing appropriately goes a long way in making a good first impression. Even if you see employees or other interns doing certain things, don't always be so quick to follow their lead. Here are 20 things you can do to make sure you get noticed for the right things:

1. Take it seriously. Treat your internship like your first professional job.
2. Don't wear headphones, a hat, or shades around the office.
3. Dress for success. You may have heard the saying, "Dress for the job you want, not the one you have."
4. Be on time. If an emergency comes up, call and let your manager know you will be late. Be on time not just to get to work but for every meeting and event you attend.
5. Always take a notepad and a pen into every meeting even if you think it will only last two minutes.
6. Never take your cell phone to a meeting and while at your desk don't constantly text/tweet/post on your phone or computer. If you need to keep time, buy a watch.

7. If you break rule number six, don't check your phone at all during the meeting.

8. Listen and learn about the company and the industry so that you can ask interesting questions that demonstrate your interest in the company and/or industry. Stay aware by reading industry publications, company reports, and other materials that can help you stand out amongst others.

9. If you are given an assignment you don't understand, ask questions rather than do it wrong.

10. Be organized and learn to manage your time wisely. You can use systems like Evernote, an app on your phone, or good old-fashioned pen and paper. Whatever system you use, learn to manage your time.

11. If you find yourself with nothing to do ask for additional assignments that you can assist with. You don't want to be seen with idle time just hanging around. Ask your manager if there are any new projects you can take on, or you may have a suggestion for a new project if you've completed all of the others. If your manager doesn't have any new assignments, ask if it is appropriate to seek out an assignment from someone else in the department.

12. Periodically ask for feedback on your work and performance. Understand that your manager will

not have time for lengthy meetings every day to discuss how you are doing. If you would like some feedback, ask to schedule a meeting every 1-2 weeks to discuss your projects.

13. Get your work done before you socialize. Get to know the folks in your office and the other interns but don't be in a rush to over share. You don't want to get pulled into gossip or be the intern who is never at their desk because they are chatting someone up.

14. Men should keep a necktie in their desk drawer and ladies a nice pair of heels because you might just get invited to a lunch or dinner meeting with the boss, or asked to attend a networking event at the last minute. Men and women should keep a blazer or sport coat handy as well.

15. Network. This word keeps coming up so it must be important. Internships provide a tremendous opportunity to build a network with working professionals.

16. Find a mentor. Good mentors can be instrumental in your future success.

17. Raise your hand to take on projects and show initiative, but don't raise your hand for every project. Avoid getting overloaded to the point that your work suffers, but do challenge yourself. You want to show initiative, but you also want to produce quality work. In this case, quality over

quantity is key.

18. Pay attention to detail. If you are working on a project, take your time to review it when it is complete before you submit it. Proofread your work and recheck your calculations, then do it again. You want to avoid careless errors that could easily have been prevented.

19. Remain teachable. No one of us is perfect so there will be a time when you get feedback that you did something wrong. When you get feedback on a project, do not take it to heart as criticism but as a learning opportunity. Ask questions so that you can learn how you can be better at the next opportunity.

20. Stay in touch. When your internship is coming to a close, ask those who you worked well with if you can connect on LinkedIn.

Nine

NETWORKING DOESN'T HAVE TO BE AWKWARD

What do you think when you hear the word networking? Do you imagine standing alone in a room full of people trying to not look awkward? Does networking mean trying to meet someone with the sole interest of getting them to give you a job? That approach and attitude can derail your networking success before you even get started.

The Miriam-Webster Dictionary defines networking as, *the exchange of information or services among individuals, groups, or institutions; specifically: the cultivation of productive relationships for employment or business.* Networking is connecting; it is helping; it is relating and being a resource.

As a college student, networking is something you should grow comfortable with. Moving into your professional career, networking will be something that you engage in for a very long time. Even at this stage of the game for you, networking is going to open up opportunities for you. "I think every student should do at least one internship before graduating. I am finishing up my second internship right now and will be able to stay with the organization after graduation if I don't secure a full-time job right away. Interning is a great way to network and see what field of study is actually for you," says Jalen McGill, a senior at the SUNY College

---

If you can become successful at building and maintaining relationships, you will find that more opportunities will come to you. Those relationships can lead to promotions, recommendations, or even job offers.

---

at Brockport, majoring in Sports Management. He found his current internship with the Rochester RazorSharks basketball team through networking.

If you can become successful at building and maintaining relationships, you will find that more opportunities will come to you. Those relationships can lead to promotions, recommendations, or even job offers. Those relationships also position you to be a resource for others. The further you go in your career, the larger and more influential your network becomes. As you can tap into that expanded network, you can become an ever greater giver as you learn to connect people to each other. That is when you have really started to capture the essence of networking, when you serve to be a resource and not just look for your own opportunities. If you keep that mindset you will have a better experience in building relationships because your attitude and approach will come from a more pure place internally.

There will be many types of networking activities that you can and will engage in. Networking events are not always formal events at bars or restaurants or cocktail hours. The opportunity to network can present itself at a company outing, a company party, or even a company volunteer day. You could find yourself sitting in line for coffee or riding the elevator with someone you've been trying to connect with at your internship. No matter the situation, what do you plan to say while networking? How will you present yourself? How do you break the ice? How do you join a group already having a conversation? As with most things, the more you practice the more natural some of these scenarios will be for you. You will be able to understand more about yourself, you will get more comfortable, and you will be able to better identify opportunity.

Networking Events

As you begin to intern in corporate environments and join professional organizations, you will have the opportunity to network outside of the office. You will find yourself at networking events, holiday parties, conferences, workshops, volunteer days, company softball games, and other formal and informal gatherings. It is essential that you learn how to introduce yourself, start and join conversations. Have you ever heard of an elevator pitch? An elevator pitch is a 30 second introductory speech about your strengths, interests, skills, and goals. The concept is based on the idea that if you stepped into an elevator with the exact person you were trying to meet and all you have is the elevator ride (30 seconds or less) to make them interested in speaking with you more, what would you say? How can you sell yourself effectively in that short timeframe?

The 30-second elevator pitch can help you break the ice and feel a little more relaxed in intimidating environments. Your pitch should be memorable, interesting, and concise. By the end of your pitch, the listener should know who you are, what you do, the type of opportunity you are looking for, and what you bring to the table. The uses of an elevator pitch extend beyond just networking situations but at career fairs as well. It can also be used in a job interview when the interviewer says, "Tell me about yourself?" With some adjustment you can take the same content and effectively answer that question in a precise and succinct manner. You can also adapt your pitch to be included in your cover letter or introductory email.

As you sit down to begin crafting your pitch, you can follow a simple formula to writing an effective pitch. Start with the basics. Be sure to include your name, school, major, and class year. Since you will primarily be at your internship you should craft your initial pitch to be used in that environment. You want to ensure that you include your internship department and position along with your other basic information. Moving further into the pitch, you can share briefly about what you are doing at your internship and what you are interested in doing next. If you are a graduating senior, take this chance to mention what you are looking to do after you graduate.

Take some time to list out the projects you are working on and summarize them. Examine your contributions to those projects and find the highlights that you can share in your brief summary. To explain what you are interested in doing, you have to know exactly that. Think about what it is you are looking for next and how your current internship connects you to that future. This is also the place to mention other projects, internships, or leadership activities that you have participated in as well. The key is learning how to tie it all together and make it flow—in about 30 seconds.

When you get to the closing, you have to finish strong. Finish with an engaging statement or question. At your internship site, the end of your pitch is a perfect opportunity to ask for the opportunity to conduct an informational interview. When you speak, convey passion, enthusiasm, and confidence and of course while you do so, you must smile.

Sample 1

"Hi, my name is Sharise. This fall I will be a senior at XYZ University where I'm studying public relations. As a corporate communications intern here, I've been writing press releases, pitching stories to local media, and conducting research for upcoming projects. I've been able to enhance my writing skills and understand the art of pitching to media. I'd love to do an informational interview with you about your experiences with the company because it has been such a learning experience so far."

Sample 2

"Hi, my name is Sharise. I am an intern in the

Finance department this summer. I just graduated from XYZ University with a degree in finance. This is my third finance internship, my first two where with investment firms but I've enjoyed the ability to get into more revenue analysis, budgeting, and developing reports here. After my internship I'd love to start my career here. If you have time, I'd really appreciate the chance to do an informational interview with you about how you've been able to build a successful career with this company."

Practice your elevator pitch in the mirror, with friends, and with anyone who can give you honest feedback. Work on delivering your pitch with good energy and at a steady pace that doesn't sound overly rehearsed. After you find your style and gain comfort you can practice adjusting your pitch to difference situations and environments. It may seem like I keep telling you to visit career services (because I do), but they are there to offer you assistance for free. They can help you craft your pitch and give you valuable feedback and tips for improvement. Sometimes they can provide you with a video recording so that you can see yourself, which can really aid in your improvement as an interviewee.

Don't think that your elevator pitch will always be the lead in for every introduction. Networking is also simply about having conversations. If you see someone in line in the company lunchroom with a hat of your favorite sports team, make a comment because that person could be a fan as well. Perhaps you are riding the elevator with someone with really nice shoes, just tell the person. You don't have to always try and be super creative to start a conversation; sometimes a genuine compliment or question can open the door enough to get to your elevator pitch.

Informational Interviews

Many working professionals are willing to share experiences with current students. They have been where you are and the opportunity to provide a little insight into how to succeed is something that they will gladly share. After you graduate, it is a little harder to secure face-to-face time. To take full advantage of picking the brains of people who are where you want to be, informational interviews are the way to go. During your internship, I want you to consider it as a requirement that you set for yourself to complete at least two informational interviews.

An informational interview is a one-on-one interview you conduct with a professional to learn about a career and profession that you are interested in. It is the perfect opportunity to learn about what it takes to succeed in an industry, what the day-to-day life is like in that career, and how you can get started. Informational interviews provide you with a wealth of information about potential career paths and provide professional connections. This is an opportunity for you to research, listen, and learn so that you can understand how to position yourself for success. Go in with that mindset and you will have a more successful interview experience. It could also be the opportunity to identify a mentor. It doesn't matter if you are interning at a company with 10 or 10,000 employees, there will be someone that you can connect with and learn from.

Although it is not a formal job interview, if you conduct yourself in a manner that is impressive, it could lead to future job considerations. Participating in these interviews will give you more confidence in the interviewing process, as you ask and answer questions in a less intimidating environment. Sometime it could be a conversation over lunch based on the person's availability.

Getting the Informational Interview

Unless you make the effort to learn how to get an informational interview you obviously won't be able to conduct one. There are a few methods you can use to proceed in securing an informational interview. Being an intern creates an avenue to access the contacts to get interviews done.

You can start within your internship department. After you've gotten settled into your internship, you can ask your manager if you can take a few minutes per week to have informational interviews with various members of the team. You don't want to try and take the time spent working on projects with staff to cram in an information interview. You want to set up and schedule a time so that you both know exclusively what the conversation will be about.

Getting an interview with people in other departments will be beneficial as well. You can learn how different departments within the same company can operate and explore new careers you may not have thought about. Some companies will be more supportive of your efforts to learn about careers and might even encourage you to set up your interviews. Other companies might not be as open and supportive. If you meet resistance or there is concern about interviews interfering with your work, you can use your lunchtime to conduct them. If you are scheduling the interview with someone you see daily in your department the process will be slightly less intimidating. You can send them an email and ask to have some time to speak.

On the day of your interview, if you are already at your internship you should of course already be dressed professionally. If your office allows you to dress business casual, you may want to step it up a little that day to more formal business attire. Arrive a few minutes early and have your questions prepared. When you walk into the office, feel free to provide them with a copy of your resume. This is not so that they can immediately offer you a job, but so that you can get advice from them about what you can include or delete from it when applying to a role in their field. By taking a look at your experiences, it allows them to get a sense of where you are and advise you better on how you might stack up against other competition.

Sample Email (in office)

Hi Tim _____,

I'm really enjoying my internship thus far. In my first two weeks I've already had the chance to work on a major presentation for the sales team. The team has been very welcoming and I appreciate the opportunity to be here. If you are available, I would like to schedule an informational interview with you to learn more about your role and how you have gotten to where you are so far in your career. Are you available on Tuesday at 11:30 a.m.?

Thanks,

_____

Sample Email

Hello _____,

I am interning in the marketing department here at YXZ company this summer. It has been a great experience thus far. In my first two weeks, I've already had the chance to work on a major presentation for the sales team. I know the remaining weeks will be just as interesting.

I am a rising junior at XYZ University majoring in Psychology and I hope to pursue a career in market research or sales when I graduate. I would appreciate the opportunity to ask you a few questions about your career path in Marketing and learn what advice you have for a young professional desiring to succeed in this industry.

Please let me know if you are available for a meeting in person over the next few weeks while I am here. I am in the office every day so I can work around your schedule to find a mutually agreeable time to chat.

Thank you for your time and I look forward to speaking with you.

Sincerely,

_____

Questions to Ask

Once you have secured an interview and scheduled a time to speak, what should you discuss? This is a chance to ask questions, learn, and most importantly listen. Take advantage of this situation to ask a few questions that you wouldn't normally ask in a regular job interview; there is slightly more latitude to tactfully discuss things like salary and lifestyle. Your questions can range from questions about work environment, their personal career path, the company, the industry, and the day-to-day role to expect in the position.

Here are 21 questions you can consider to ask in your interview. You will not have the time to go over them all. Informational interviews last 15-30 minutes dependent upon the person's time. Don't just follow this list in order but arrange the questions the best you see fit to make sure you have time to get those that are most important to you answered. As always, go online and do research to gather other questions you can ask and formulate your own according to what you'd like to learn.

1. How did you find your first job after college?
2. How did you get from your first job to where you are now?

3. What is the best advice you can offer me to succeed in this industry?
4. What are some industry publications that you can recommend that I read or professional organizations I should join?
5. What are the growth opportunities you see in this field?
6. What is your typical workday like?
7. What are the most rewarding and difficult parts of your job?
8. How has and will technology influence your job?
9. What are the greatest pressures you face in your role?
10. What skills are necessary to advance in this field?
11. Is graduate school necessary to advance in this industry?
12. Can you recommend courses or activities I should engage in before I graduate that will make me a stronger candidate for entry into this field.
13. What are the main or most important personal characteristics for success in the field?
14. What are the different settings in this field where I can pursue a career (i.e., academic institutions, banks, non-profits, etc.)?
15. Do you find this position to be demanding on your time outside of the office?
16. Does a career in this field allow for a lot of flexibility, or can I expect to have a pretty

standard set schedule?

17. How should I go about looking for an entry-level job in this field?
18. What type of salary can I expect at the entry-level in this field, and where might I be ten years into the profession?
19. Why did you choose to work for this company?
20. What are the qualities or characteristics I should look for in a company to work for?

At the conclusion of your interview your final questions could be, "Do you know anyone else who might be willing to talk to me? May I say that you referred me?" That would be a way for you to continue learning more about the industry and making additional connections. You also want to ask if you can stay in touch with them. That leaves the door open to build a relationship for a future reference or a mentor.

Follow Up

When the interview is over, you want to send a thank you note or email. If they connected you to another contact, this would be the perfect time to let them know the result of that effort as well. Your note does not need to be lengthy, it is just to show them that you truly valued the time they took to speak with you. Handwritten notes still show that you went the extra step.

Sample Thank You

Hello _____,

Thank you for taking the time to speak with me Friday. I thoroughly enjoyed our conversation and appreciate your willingness to share your experiences with me. Our conversation has fueled my interest and desire to be successful in this field, and your advice has given me a lot to consider. As I start my job search, I hope that I will be writing soon to let you know that I have landed a position.

Sincerely,
Student X

Keeping In Contact

Just as important as making contact through networking and informational interviewing, is maintaining those contacts. Don't do the work of reaching out to people and making a connection, only to not follow up and keep the connection going.

Maintaining connections with your contacts doesn't have to be an overwhelmingly complex and time-consuming task.

Keeping in touch is important so that your network knows what is happening with you and so that you know what is happening with people in your network. No one appreciates only being called upon when you need a reference or want something from them. If you maintain genuine contact, it will be less intimidating to ask a favor of someone. Also, keeping in contact allows people to think of you for opportunities that come across their way.

Connecting professionally on LinkedIn is a great start. As your professional network grows into the hundreds, using sites like LinkedIn to make announcements about changes in life is convenient and easy. There will, however, always be a select group of mentors and managers that you will want to make more of a concerted effort to connect with personally by email or phone. Holiday's and other special occasions present an opportunity to say hello as well by sending a holiday card or even a small gift. If you get a new job or relocate that can be a time to keep your networks in the loop and update them on your move. Overall, try to connect with your main list every three to six months.

When I gave birth to my son, I received a lot of social media posts and congratulatory comments from my former students and colleagues. There were others who took the time to send personal emails and yet others who sent cards. While every post or message was appreciated, I remember best the personal well wishes that were sent via email or greeting card.

You may not be aware of those intimate details about some peoples' lives. It is important to pay attention during your conversations and take note of things that can be gateway opportunities to stay in touch. If you are doing an informational interview in someone's office and you notice sports memorabilia, it can open a brief conversation about sports and a shared common interest. Later on perhaps their favorite team wins a championship. The next day after the game would be a great time to send an email and say:

Hi John,

I know you're a big Ravens sports fan so today must be pretty awesome. I hope you enjoyed the game and enjoy being the champs for now. Next season my Buffalo Bills are coming to win the Superbowl!

Staying connected is simple. If you know someone likes to cook different types of foods and you come across an interesting recipe, share it with them; or maybe they like to travel and you read an article about the top ten travel destinations, you can send them the link. What those small gestures illustrate is that you paid attention and you cared enough to notice. You weren't asking for anything but rather just taking the opportunity to stay in touch.

Finding a Mentor

Having a good mentor can be a difference maker in your career. I've had several mentors along the way and still do. With every career move I've made, I've always sought counsel of my mentors first. Their experience and ability to see things through a different lens, as well as knowledge of me personally, always makes for informed opinions that I trust. Overtime, I have gained new mentors and become a mentor to others myself.

Depending on the company you intern with, you might be assigned a mentor from within the company. If you are participating in a non-profit internship program that places students with various companies, you may obtain a mentor through that program as well. Being connected in this capacity is great because it sets the expectation for the relationship from the beginning. You don't have to ask, they have volunteered to be your mentor. But, what if you don't get assistance from either of those sources? How do you go about finding a good mentor?

Start with your university career services or alumni office. It is possible that they have program that matches alumni with current students seeking mentors. Finding a mentor through an alumni network gives you common ground to start from. Alumni are often motivated to help others who have come from the same path and share an affinity for a college that provided them with education and experiences to launch their own careers.

If you have joined a professional organization with campus chapters, then you could seek out a mentor through the organization and your chapter advisor. Maybe you have a good friend with a parent or family member that is working in the career you aspire to pursue and they can become your mentor. You can also check with your fraternity or sorority or religious group to get connected to others who can serve as mentors for you. Through networking at your internship and your informational interviews, as you build relationships with those contacts they also become people who can become mentors.

Will You Be My Mentor?

If you haven't been set up with a mentor through a program, then you should formally ask a person to be your mentor. Set up a time to call the person, or if possible visit with the person face to face. You are going to be asking them to become vested in your success and spend valuable time helping you reach your goals. Writing an email to set up the meeting is okay, but this conversation is one that is best had in-person or over the phone (Skype is okay too) if possible.

During your meeting, you want to express your desire for them to serve as your mentor and why. Perhaps they have the job and have followed a career path that you would like to emulate. If they don't work in your field, you may admire their overall business savvy and come from similar backgrounds. Your mentor doesn't have to be a professional with 30 years of experience; don't overlook what a young professional three to five years into their career can share with you as well.

Outline your goals and expectations for the relationship so that you are both clear. You can establish a regular meeting schedule and create guidelines for communications in between. Being respectful of their time; don't expect to have weekly meetings. Talking once a month or every other month for 30-60 minutes is enough to keep you both engaged in the relationship. Having a regular meeting schedule can help you come up with questions and topics that you want to discuss so you can maximize your time and theirs. As time goes on it may not be necessary to have the regularly scheduled meetings on a frequent basis. You may find that you speak a few times a year and the conversation is both professional and personal, as this person has been vested in your success on many levels.

Ten

THE END IS JUST THE BEGINNING

As your internship starts to whine down, you don't want to limp to the finish line, rather you want to finish strong. By strong finish, I mean keep coming in on time, dressing professionally, remaining attentive, and asking questions up until the very end. Finishing strong is not only the responsible thing to do, but it is the impression that you want to leave on the folks you are leaving behind. Take the last two weeks to conduct your final few informational interviews, finish up any projects and presentations, and begin securing recommendations and your mentor (if you have someone you want to ask).

At the start of your last two weeks, ask for a letter of recommendation. You don't want to wait until the last few days because the person you are asking is no doubt busy. If you wait too late to ask, you may not get it before the internship is over. Two weeks gives your writer the time to think and compose a more thoughtful letter. Your last week is also the time to begin ensuring you have the right contact information for the people in your department. Reach out to those you want to maintain contact with on LinkedIn and transfer their contact information from your work email to your personal email.

One of the last activities you should engage in is writing thank you notes. Buying a pack of blank thank you cards and writing personal notes to each member of the team you work with can go a long way in

---

The internship process is not just about adding work experience to you resume, it is about the journey of self-discovery and finding where you want to fit professionally.

---

cementing your place as a rock-star intern in their minds. Make it personal with each note by commenting on how they have helped you over the internship period.

Many companies conduct an end of internship evaluation for your benefit as well as their own. Do not be intimidated by this, embrace it as a learning experience. You get to have direct feedback about your performance and learn what you are great at as well as what you need to improve on. You can take that information and get better at whatever skill you are lacking so that you can be an even more confident candidate. If you don't get any negative feedback, then continue to improve on the things you are already doing well until they are perfected. Usually, there is something that they can share with you to improve on. If your internship site does not have a formal evaluation process, then ask to meet with your direct supervisor towards the end of your internship and ask for feedback on your performance. Schedule the meeting so that they can have time to consider their answers and not just try and think of things on the spot.

It is also important that beyond the official or unofficial evaluation completed by your supervisor, is your ability to self-evaluate. Ask yourself what you liked about the experience and could you see yourself doing that job every day. What did you learn by observing the people in the field and their lives? Out of my eight internship experiences, I enjoyed some more than others. I learned just as much about what I wanted in a career versus what I didn't want. For me, some of the observations I came away with over time included that I didn't want to be in an office all day, every day; I wanted a position that would allow me to travel and that I did better in situations where I felt I was making an impact on people personally.

You might discover that you love the structure and

resources of a big company and the defined career paths or that you would prefer the entrepreneurial environment of a smaller start up. You may find that you love wearing a suit every day and the corporate office environment or you might figure out that you prefer a more casual work environment. Ultimately, you may find that the career you thought you'd love isn't what you thought it was. It could be that you just need to find a different environment or it could mean that you have to consider carefully the track you want to stay on.

The internship process is not just about adding work experience to your resume, it is about the journey of self-discovery and finding where you want to fit professionally. Don't look at it as just a work experience; consider it to be a life experience. You should come away knowing that you spent time doing something that has given you a greater sense of discovery and direction for your career path. It totally may not be what you imagined it to be, but that still means it has added value to your life. Even if you hated the internship, embrace that it was over in a few weeks and that if that were your post-college life, you might have had to endure it longer. Take that negative experience and set out to find the next internship or job, knowing better what you don't want to be a part of.

Did I Get the Job?

An internship is almost like an extended job interview—much extended. For a few weeks or months an employer gets to observe you and see how you contribute, your quality of work, how you handle pressure, and if you are a good fit for their team and company. They see your habits, your strengths, and weaknesses. At the end of it all, if you are a graduating senior you could have a job offer.

Many companies go into the internship season with the expectation that they will hire a set number of new employees from their interns. Other companies take it as it goes. During the interview stage it is good to ask if they plan to hire interns for full-time openings at the end of the internship. Even if they say no, it shouldn't impact your performance. You never know when a person might quit and they all of a sudden have an opening. If you start strong and stay strong through the internship, you might get the opportunity to fill an unexpected role. If you are returning to school, your stellar performance could earn you an offer to return back to intern with them again. Every year, a few of the companies I worked with would contact me inquiring about an intern they had the previous year, and if they were available to intern again.

If you do an outstanding job (as a graduating senior

doing an internship) and are not offered the job, do not take it personal. Sometimes there just isn't room in the budget. If you have done a great job, the company will likely not hesitate to give you an outstanding recommendation. Also, they may not have an opening at that exact moment but if you keep the lines of communication open and let them know you are interested in working there, they could call you in the future.

I met Eric Petit-Frere during the fall of 2011 when he'd just started his junior year at Howard University. He came to the T. Howard Foundation office to participate in the interview phase to see if he would earn a spot with the internship program. During our interview I was very impressed with his focus, professionalism, and sincerity. He scored high marks on the interview and was admitted to the program.

During the placement process I received a request for an intern to work in Production for DIRECTV in Los Angeles, CA. Eric had the right background, met the GPA requirements, and possessed a great working knowledge of production. I reached out to him to discuss the internship and then sent his resume forward. He interviewed for the internship and was offered the placement from DIRECTV.

Prior to the start of his internship he, along with the other interns in the T. Howard program, attended an Orientation program designed to prepare students for their corporate internship experience. "When it came to the Orientation and the help I received from Sharise, it really helped find tune my skills to enter the field properly," stated Eric.

He spent his summer before his senior year in Los Angeles supporting live production events like Wimbledon and the PGA Championship and studio operations for shows including the Dan Patrick Show for DIRECTV. For Eric, interning in LA was also about getting out of his comfort zone. Being from New York City and attending college in Washington, DC, moving to the west coast for the summer was a part of the learning experience as well. At the end of his internship, I received a call from the internship coordinator who was over the moon ecstatic with how well Eric had performed during the internship. What was especially impressive was his end of summer presentation, which he'd presented flawlessly. When I spoke with Eric in regards to how he felt about his internship, he had high praise for the company and his entire experience he had as well.

In the fall of his senior year, Eric returned to Howard University to complete his Bachelor's degree in Radio, TV & Film. Like most students, he was considering his future—if he would go into the workforce or should he go to graduate school, where would he live, and the other questions seniors are faced with. His plans materialized during the fall of his senior year when he received a call from DIRECTV offering him a position as a Production Operator. He gladly accepted his first job before he even got halfway through his senior year. Not only would he have a job waiting for him upon graduation but the company was also generous enough to assist him with his cross country move from Washington, DC to Los Angeles. Eric didn't have to go through additional multiple interviews to get the job. The 12-week internship he completed was enough for DIRECTIV to know they wanted him on their team.

Finish strong. You don't know who is watching and what opportunities will come.

Eleven
DIVERSITY

Diversity in the workplace happens in a variety of ways. You will no doubt encounter people from various backgrounds, geographic areas, socioeconomic status', genders, sexual orientations, religious beliefs, ethnic groups, race, age, and even educational level. Based on your own personal experiences you may or may not have been widely exposed to a large variety of people groups. If you have grown up in a relatively homogenous environment, moving into a corporate internship or any internship at a company comprised of people not seemingly like yourself, can be a difficult transition.

I want to speak for a moment specifically about racial and gender diversity in the work place. Minority students and women entering many environments may not find many people that physically represent their people group when they look around. It can be an intimidating prospect to find yourself as the only minority amongst an entire office of non-minority coworkers or only woman in a male dominated place. For some, these situations can seem intimidating and make you feel as though you are under a microscope. The unfortunate reality is that often times, there will be certain people who pay more attention to your work than other interns, because they have bought into stereotypes based on race or ethnicity, gender, and ignorance.

Your performance as an impressive intern could pave the way and assist in debunking some untruths that others may have formed based on their own limited interactions with people from other backgrounds.

If you find yourself in that scenario, the best thing you can do is perform, and perform well. Your performance as an impressive intern could pave the way and assist in debunking some untruths that others may have formed based on their own limited interactions with people from other backgrounds.

On more than one occasion, I was the only brown face in an office or department. When working at my first internship for the Red Wings professional baseball team, I was one of two female interns working with eleven male interns, and an office full of other men. I did not let the environment distract me from getting the job done. My goal remained first and foremost, to stand out. Stand out not because I may have been the only person of color in the office, or one of only a few women, but stand out because it was my intention to outperform everyone else.

If you find yourself in a hostile or insensitive work environment, know that just because you are an intern does not mean that you have to tolerate insensitive comments about your race, gender, ethnicity, sexuality, religion, age, or other difference. Some comments may be made out of ignorance. If someone makes a comment that you find offensive, and you feel comfortable in doing so, take the opportunity to bring it to their attention in a subtle way. It does not have to be done in an embarrassing manner for either of you.

If approached with a question that you deem to be insensitive or ignorant, you can simply reply in a non-confrontational manner. "That's interesting. Is there any particular way that you arrived at that conclusion?" There are times when some people just need to be encouraged to consider the origin of their comments. If the person did not intentionally mean any harm, they will consider carefully where their comment came from and maybe even apologize. If the intent was malicious, it may at least give them pause before coming at you again with another comment. There are so many scenarios that you can face as a woman or minority in a work place setting that I am not able to cover them all. Have confidence, exceed expectations, and remain professional through every encounter.

Those challenging situations are also where having a mentor or the support of an internship program is a benefit. You could call and explain the situation and seek the advice of a working professional that you trust before moving forward. Your mentor could be able to provide some context of the comment or form an appropriate response. Also, it might be helpful to have an outside objective and professional ear, before escalating any issues to a management level.

If you feel as though you are being bullied or that someone is intentionally continuously making comments, you should speak with your supervisor. If the offender is your supervisor, you should seek out the assistance of the human resources department.

I cannot promise that taking issues of diversity, discrimination, or abuse to a superior won't result in some backlash. While discrimination of any type is not legal, it is an unfortunate part of life in corporate America that many people encounter. That does not mean that if you are wronged you shouldn't stand up for yourself, but I won't sugarcoat things and say that there may not be negative reactions on the part of others. You have to weigh each battle for yourself, and also the length of time you will be there. I encourage you to embrace the diversity that exists across racial lines and seek out opportunities to learn about other cultures, practices, and even embrace diversity of thought.

Twelve
ACTION TAKERS

A degree alone is not enough anymore. The job market continues to be competitive for each new class of graduates. While you are still in school, it is your responsibility to do everything you can to gain a competitive edge. Internships are a necessary part of gaining that edge and letting you separate yourself from the pack. Don't stop at just one, do as many internships as possible.

This manual is your step-by-step guide to making your dream internship happen. All of what you have read will be worthless if you fail to take action. A few keys to your internship and eventual career success rest with your ability to take action, be a go getter, and not wait for opportunity to drop into your lap. Make it your mission to get your dream internship this (or next) summer and then make it your mission to excel.

Earlier in this book we discussed the cycles for applying for internships. If it is summer right now, you can get started today looking for fall internships. Some companies begin posting their fall internships starting as early as June.

If you happen to complete this book during the fall, then you should be setting your sights on a summer internship. Companies begin posting summer internship openings as early as November. In your

---

I challenge you to challenge yourself. Take your newly acquired knowledge of goal setting and plot your path to success.

---

desire to secure a summer internship, don't forget that during the fall semester you can also simultaneously search for a spring internship as well. No matter what time of year it is right now, you have the ability to move and take action towards your dream internship starting today.

I challenge you to challenge yourself. Take your newly acquired knowledge of goal setting and plot your path to success. Get your tools in gear and seek out professional guidance to create your best resume. Participate in mock interviews and learn how to appear confident and capable. Armed with the proper tools, your search process will be efficient and effective. The goal isn't, however, just to do a good job searching for an internship, but to get your dream internship. When that goal is achieved, the next goal is to shine bright at that internship.

As a current student or recent graduate, you are on the verge of launching your career. Embrace internships as an extension of your college education. Internships also allow you to learn what to expect when you join the workforce and prepare you for real life work place scenarios. Ask questions, be a sponge, and learn all that you can. At the end of each experience, you will be stronger, wiser, and closer to your dream career. Intern early, and intern often.

APPENDIX
Sample Resumes

Happy Student

123 Main St., College, NY 12345
hstudent.1@internmanal.com
(123) 555-5555

EDUCATION
University of Internships (UI), New York, NY   Expected
Grad: May 2016
Bachelor of Arts, Communications
Cumulative GPA: 3.77

HONORS/AWARDS
Gates Millennium Scholar, Dean's list 2014-2015

RELEVANT COURSES
Public Relations Writing, Statistics, Marketing, Spanish IV

EXTRACURRICULAR / LEADERSHIP ACTIVITIES
American Marketing Association, UI Campus Chapter Sept 2015 – Present
Chapter President
- Responsible for managing chapter meetings
- Oversee six person executive board
- Increased monthly meeting attendance from 20 to 45 by creating special series featuring local marketing professionals

University of Internships, NY, NY
Sept 2014 – May 2015
Resident Assistant
- Developed a sense of community through facilitating and organizing monthly events
- Created and maintained Facebook group page for residence hall to post events and promote dialogue among residents
- Met with residents to intervene and negotiate conflicts

- Enforced rules and conduct according to the Office of Residence Life standards

CollegeBound, NY, NY
May 2013 – Aug 2013
Mentor/Counselor
- Spoke to high school students about college experience
- Assisted students in college application process
- Read college students applications essays and provided feedback

SKILLS
Technical: Advanced proficiency in Microsoft (Word, PowerPoint, and Outlook); Adobe Photoshop; Facebook
Language: Advanced Spanish (reading and writing)

Intern L. Student

123 Main St., College, NY 12345 | (555) 555-4444
hstudent.1@internmanal.com | linkedinprofile.com

EDUCATION

University of Internships (UI), New York, NY
Expected Grad: May 2016
Bachelor of Arts   Cumulative GPA: 3.79
Major: Advertising **Minor**: Digital Media

RELEVANT COURSES: Principles of Advertising, Advertising Design, Accounting Principles, Digital Media Production

INTERNSHIP EXPERIENCE

Career Services Office, UI, NY, NY   May 2014 –
May 2015
Career Assistant
- Created two-minute commercial advertising annual career fair on campus
- Served as a greeter for employers attending the annual career fair
- Managed Facebook and Twitter accounts for career services office
- Increased Twitter following of career services page from 1,000 to 2,000 in six months

Enterprise Rent-a-Car, Brooklyn, NY
Sept 2014 – Dec 2014
Management Trainee Intern
- Accompanied store manager on business development meetings to prospective clients
- Assisted customers with selecting rental vehicle and explained rental contract
- Consistently met store goal of selling rental insurance to 15% of renters

LEADERSHIP ACTIVITIES

University of Internships, NY, NY

June 2014 – Sept 2014

Orientation Leader

- Serve as a resource to incoming students and families to aid in transition to UI
- Demonstrate knowledge of campus and community resources by giving new arrivals campus tours
- Promote interaction and team-building among new students through facilitating group activities and icebreakers

SKILLS

Technical: Advanced proficiency in Microsoft (Word, PowerPoint, and Excel); Adobe Photoshop; Facebook; Wordpress. Intermediate proficiency in HTML

GOOD L. STUDENT

123 Main Street, Rochester, NY 14619 | 585-555-5555
internmanual@gmail.com | linkedinprofile.com

EDUCATION

The College at Brockport (SUNY) – Brockport, NY
May 2015
Bachelor of Arts, <u>Major</u>: Sports Management   <u>Minor</u>:
Marketing

Relevant Courses: Principles of Marketing, Sports Marketing,
Sports and Society, Accounting
Principles, Intro to Finance

INTERNSHIP EXPERIENCE

Rochester Red Wings | Rochester, NY   Dec
2014 – Present
Community Relations Intern

- Coordinated and regulated player appearances at various
  non-profit organizations in the community
- Arranged and attended community events encouraging
  healthy eating and living, the importance of physical
  activity and education
- Networked and contacted members of the community
  regarding participation in national anthem and half time
  performances

YMCA | Rochester NY   May
2014 – Dec 2014
Event Planning Intern

- Hosted monthly educational programs for senior citizens
  about health and wellness issues
- Created and arranged monthly events for senior citizens in
  the neighborhood
- Created and managed Facebook page promoting annual
  Adopt-A-Senior event

200

WORK EXPERIENCE

DollarTree | Rochester, NY
Jan 2013 – Dec 2013
Assistant Manager
- Responsible for opening and closing store and making bank deposits
- Trained new cashiers on using cash register and conducting credit transactions
- Supervised staff of 3-6 cashiers when store manager was not available

EXTRACURRICULAR ACTIVITIES

Intramural Flag Football, *Team Captain* | SUNY Brockport Sept 2013 – Dec 2013
Sports Management Association, *Marketing Manager* | SUNY Brockport   Jan 2014 – May 2014
National Association of Black Accountants, *Member* | SUNY Brockport   Sept 2014 – May 2015

COMPUTER SKILLS

Advanced in Microsoft Word, Excel & PowerPoint
Social Media: Facebook, Twitter

ACKNOWLEDGEMENTS

I would like to thank my parents, Verline and Nathan, for setting the example of hard work and dedication, and my family for their continued support and encouragement.

Big thanks to my husband, Charles for being my biggest cheerleader, supporter and sounding board during this process, and for believing in me at times more than I believed in myself. Love you.

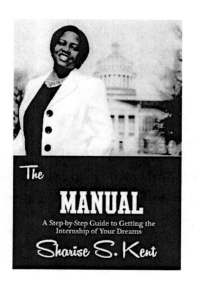

Want more information? Visit
www.theinternshipmanual.com
for additional resources, including a
FREE Internship Manual Toolkit!